THIS IS THE ANSWER

ADVICE FOR NEW ENTREPRENEURS FROM THE WORLD'S WORST BUSINESS COACH

DAN NORRIS

Published by Dan Norris
http://dannorris.me
The moral right of the author has been asserted.

First Printing, 2019

Cataloguing-in-Publication entry is available from the National Library of Australia.

ISBN: 978-1-64184-094-1 (paperback)
ISBN: 978-1-64184-095-8 (ebook)

CONTENTS

FOREWORD

If I needed to get some big influencer to endorse
this, the book would make no sense. Read on.

INTRODUCTION

Wearing a tailored black pinstripe suit and red tie, TJ Jones stands on the stage confidently with hands in front, fingers touching. It's early in the day. The audience has come to see Richard Branson but has enough patience to sit through some other speakers first. Most of them know the deal. The tickets were cheap, they are paid for by speakers trying to flog hope from stage, giving a percentage back to the organizers to help cover the fees from big-name speakers.

TJ tells the crowd about the many people he's made millionaires. He's a business coach, and the students who've bought his programs have almost universally gone on to make more than a million dollars shortly after. He shows video testimonials from past students who attribute their millions directly to TJ and his teachings.

He stops briefly to call out someone from the crowd and begins to analyse their body language, personality, and station in life. He nails most of it, impressing the crowd, gets some laughs, and moves on. His guru status is escalating in the naturally skeptical crowd.

He shows videos of him with famous rappers, more video testimonials, and then brings some past students up on stage. A short nerdy white guy, an African-American woman, an Asian businessman, and the list goes on. TJ clearly has something here that spans continents. It's a universal truth. They got the memo about the dark suit and red tie too, and it turns out most of these successful students themselves will be interviewing more celebrities at his next exclusive event. What I wouldn't give to be part of this club!

He includes a very small amount of actual content in his talk with a few general business tips, just some small things that have helped him become the multi-millionaire he is today. Those small things make great stories and provide some value, but if the members of the audience really want to become millionaires within the next twelve months, they need something more. Something that he's reserved only for his elite mastermind members. This isn't something he can share with everyone from stage. It's not that simple. It will only be available to a select few individuals, prepared to do as he and other successful business people have done, and invest in themselves.

He tells the audience he has a special offer for them and lists all of the inclusions with prices attached. Video training, email support, a free ticket to any event he ever runs from now on, membership in his community, a 1-on-1 business planning session, and the list goes on. But this isn't for everyone, he explains. Most people will self-sabotage their success. Most won't invest in themselves because they don't believe they are worthy. This is only for people who are ready to receive the answer. And not just anyone, only the first fifty who prove they believe in themselves enough to deserve it. Only those people who have a burning fire inside themselves that has never had the potential to shine.

While the total value is well into the hundreds of thousands, he offers it today only for $3,997, gestures with an open palm to the back left of the room, and tells people to run there to sign up. He keeps pitching as *Firework* by Katy Perry starts playing, and people begin to stand up. He's the last talk before the break, and with the sign-up table strategically positioned near the exit, it's impossible to know who's signing up or who's leaving to vomit in the nearest toilet.

Most of the audience will be skeptical. After all, they came to hear Richard Branson's story; they didn't come to sign up to a business mastermind. Despite that, he *will* sell those fifty tickets. He's done this many times before, and he always sells the fifty tickets. The Cialdini sales tricks

(Reciprocity, Scarcity, Authority, Consistency, Liking, Consensus), along with the NLP and the universally relatable storytelling, will be an irresistible combination for at least fifty people in the audience. The rest of the audience, if not for the understandable skepticism, might sign up as well.

Of course, if your default position is to sign up for something because a bunch of people in a room think it's a good idea, it's probably not a good idea.

We know all of these people already have businesses, and we can safely assume that they aren't going as well as they'd like.

They want to know why. Perhaps there's something TJ knows that they don't know. A secret of sorts, or just an answer to a question they've had since the day they started their business. Why are other people more successful than me?

HOW TO THINK LIKE AN ENTREPRENEUR

For whatever reason, I've always had a strong and natural cynicism towards overused, generic business advice. You know the stuff I mean: Never give up. Overcome your fears. Find a niche. Work hard. Perfect your elevator pitch. And the list goes on.

Perhaps it's the years of reading it, attempting to apply it, and realizing it doesn't work—or at least realizing that there are other ways to make things work.

But let's think about it for a minute. What exactly is an entrepreneur? According to Google, it's "A person who sets up a business or businesses, taking on financial risks in the hope of profit." I can't agree with that one. First, lots of entrepreneurs have made millions, hundreds of millions, and even billions before making a profit. Plus, are entrepreneurs really the type to "hope" for profit? I don't think so.

Perhaps Merriam-Webster can do better: "One who organizes, manages and assumes the risks of a business or enterprise." Hmm not really. Entrepreneurs start things; managers run them.

And again, Dictionary.com: "a person who organizes and manages any enterprise, especially a business, usually with considerable initiative and risk."

It's true that no one seems to be able to agree on what an entrepreneur is. But I can tell you what an entrepreneur is not, and that is someone who follows the rules or some sort of playbook. And a closer look at these three definitions reveals the key thing they agree on that is part of the deal as an entrepreneur: risk.

Entrepreneurs start things. Things that didn't exist in the same way before. Things that, by definition, don't have a playbook because they haven't been done before. Managers can follow a playbook; entrepreneurs can't. Entrepreneurs are at the forefront of risk, and they navigate their own course into the unknown.

With risk comes the potential for a big reward, which attracts a lot of people to the game. The problem is that these people are not entrepreneurs. They aren't risk takers. They want their cake, and they want to eat it too. They lap up motivational quotes and generic business advice because they want all the reward without the risk. They are looking for someone else to give them an answer instead of embracing the challenge of creating something that hasn't been created before.

Hope-driven guru advice doesn't work because there is no tried and tested path. It's a neat business model for people selling the dream, but it's not helpful to the entrepreneurs, nor is it helpful to the people who aren't sure whether they *are* entrepreneurs.

I became an entrepreneur because I couldn't handle the boredom of employment. For years, my view of what an entrepreneur was had me questioning whether I could ever be one. I was never an outgoing person. I hated sales and networking. I did poorly at business school. The signs weren't good.

It turns out being an entrepreneur isn't about having certain personality traits, and it's certainly not about following age-old blueprints. Entrepreneurship is a way of thinking. It's a chip on your shoulder. It's a mindset that says maybe the experts aren't actually right. Maybe I'll have the audacity to do the exact opposite of what everyone says to do, and if I do that enough, one time it might work.

If you want to be an entrepreneur, you can't do it by blindly following every catchy piece of business advice. You have to create your own business advice, just for you. You have to make your own hypotheses, test your own assumptions, and take your own risks.

In short, you have to think for yourself. That's what being an entrepreneur is. And with that, plus a lot of risk, a lot of trial and error, and a healthy dose of good luck and fortunate timing, you might have something. Or you might constantly fail, arriving back at the start of the process, wondering if you have it in you to start it all again.

Sound like fun? Welcome to entrepreneurship.

PERHAPS YOU SHOULD GIVE UP

I'm someone who devours their fair share of entrepreneurial content. I like books, podcasts, business movies—the whole lot. I love success and failure stories and learning from people who have gone before me in business.

But there's one thing that has always pissed me off about almost every successful person and every quote about success: the drastic overemphasis on the role of hard work and persistence.

I have always found it quite offensive that almost every successful person simply thinks that all you have to do is work hard and persist until something happens. For one thing, most of us are already working hard. But what's worse is it could be terrible advice for you. Working harder and persisting could be the opposite of what you should be doing.

What I found, after I had some success in business, is that business success is not about hard work at all. Entrepreneurs are not athletes where you can train and train and train on a specific skill and over enough time, reach mastery. Entrepreneurs live in a world of risk where one slight unpredictable act of chance can result in devastating failure or spectacular success. Successes in business often come down to a tiny moment in time where a decision is made for some reason that drastically impacts the trajectory of the business. From that point forward, momentum kicks in, and success comes far easier. The irony is that quite often that decision is to stop working hard. To stop persisting. To give up.

We are taught never to give up and to work hard, but the truth is that giving up is one of the most difficult and essential skills of any entrepreneur, and it doesn't get the attention it deserves.

When I was running my agency for seven years earning minimum wage, I worked my arse off. I hardly ever took a holiday, worked twelve-hour days most days, rarely switched off, and I had hosting customers calling me at 5:00 a.m. on my weekends regularly! I'd never worked harder in my life, but I just couldn't achieve any semblance of success with that business.

I made the extremely difficult decision to give up after seven years and start something else from scratch.

That led me to start a software business where I poured every last cent I had into it—and lost all of it. Twelve months later, again I had to make the excruciatingly difficult decision to completely give up on that, too.

That led me to start WP Curve (a WordPress support business), which turned into a million-dollar business and exit to GoDaddy a few years later.

Running WP Curve was never about hard work. I worked part-time on the business, and I earned five times as much as I'd ever earned as a wage. It grew 10% a month for two years with very little effort. That's what happens with good businesses. They grow. And momentum does a lot of the "hard work" for you.

But you will never experience it if you don't give up on ideas that don't have any momentum or any potential for momentum.

I've given up on so many ideas as an entrepreneur that it's painful to think about. I must have started 30 or 40 projects or businesses in the last 12.5 years as an entrepreneur. Almost all of them were shut down one way or another. Some I'd spent years working on and tens of thousands of dollars on. I did it again and again until I found myself in the fortunate position of having two businesses that were good.

If I kept working hard and persisting, I never would have found those businesses. I had to give up on bad ideas to open up the possibility of discovering good ideas.

Much like the pain of giving up on a relationship, it is the only way to get you to the reward of a better relationship. Working hard and persisting at trying to fix unfixable things is not productive. When you work on the wrong things, working harder and persisting is bad advice.

Giving up on ideas is still the hardest thing I have to do. Every time I get the timing wrong, I lose money. I become an emotional mess thinking about all of the effort and work I've put into something only to give up on it. And it's not just me. I see people all the time in my free Facebook group working on ideas that are just not working. I can see it, I'm sure everyone else in the group can see it, but no one says anything. I'm certain the entrepreneurs themselves even know it, but it's just such a hard thing to admit. Throw on top of that the constant glorification of failure and ongoing narrative to "keep hustling" and "never give up," and they go for years working on projects that aren't going anywhere.

Let's not sugarcoat or romanticize it. Giving up is failing, and failing fucking hurts.

For me, the projects that failed have enabled me to focus on the projects that succeeded. In almost all cases, I decide when they fail, and that's why it's so hard. But giving up and failing has enabled me to build one six-figure business and two seven-figure businesses in the last three years.

And it honestly has not been that hard. Certainly not as hard as in the early days. When momentum kicks in, things explode, and it's always been a few very small decisions that have led to momentum kicking in as opposed to years of hard work and persistence. Those small decisions are often quitting something that isn't working and starting something new that potentially could.

If you are working on something now that has no momentum, and you feel like you've given it your best shot, then perhaps you should give up.

ADVICE FROM THE WORLD'S WORST BUSINESS COACH

Over the years, hundreds if not thousands of people have come to me looking for advice on their business problems. This has particularly been the case after I saw some success building and selling WP Curve and releasing *The 7 Day Startup* and other books.

"Which logo should I use?"

"What service should I offer?"

"Should I offer this person equity and co-founder status?"

"Should I lease this space?"

"How do I sell more on Instagram?"

"Where do I find the best staff?"

The truth is, I don't like answering these questions, and I avoid them at all costs because I DON'T KNOW! Unlike business gurus who profit from selling advice, I'm not prepared to pretend I do.

There are just far too many variables. Any entrepreneur who claims to have some kind of formula for success is either delusional or dishonest or both.

I worked for seven years writing content and building a website services business with zero success. Then, in a five-minute moment of desperation, I slightly tweaked the same idea, and two years later, I had a million-dollar business and an exit to one of the biggest Internet companies on earth: GoDaddy. If I said I knew precisely how that happened, I'd be lying. But people do!

Countless entrepreneurs will share their secrets to success, and more again will offer mentorship and advisory services to entrepreneurs who need their help. People helping other people is great, but the problem arises when you as an entrepreneur think this other person has all of the answers. They don't! This is even truer when they are supremely confident that they do. The people most confident in providing you a formula for success are the ones who are least likely to be able to do it. After all, if they knew so much about business and they were obsessed entrepreneurs, they would be busy building their companies and not trying to flog ebooks or become your business coach.

By all means, learn from other people and ask for advice, but don't blindly take it. The number one person you should be taking advice from on your business is yourself. You are the one closest to the problem. You are the one who has worked on the problem more recently. You are the one who has everything on the line if you fail.

Your business problems probably don't have a simple quantifiable answer that an outsider can provide. Next time you have a challenge or a question in your business, consider this: There may not be anyone who actually knows the answer to this. This is not being pessimistic; this is becoming an entrepreneur.

I don't know the answers, but it's your job to figure them out. That's what entrepreneurs do. It's not easy; there is no simple answer or magic pill; that's why we aren't all entrepreneurs.

THE CUSTOMER IS
RARELY RIGHT

In years gone by, it made sense to whittle complex things down to simple phrases. "The customer is always right" is a great example.

The phrase was originally coined in 1909 by Harry Gordon Selfridge, the founder of Selfridges department store in London. It was a nice, quick way to send the message that customers are the most important thing to a business. But it's become much more than that. We've gotten to the point now where entrepreneurs will look to customers to solve their most complex problems. For example, many business coaches are obsessed with finding out what "your ideal customer" would say.

1909 was one year after the first production run of the Ford Model T.

All these years later, Selfridges is still in business, as is Ford (just). Quotes from that time are still around as well. The following is a popular one, despite no evidence that it was ever said:

"If I had asked people what they wanted, they would have said faster horses." Henry Ford.

It's fascinating to think that two quotes from over one hundred years ago would still be so influential today. In any case, it's worth noting that the two quotes are in direct opposition to each other. And for me, I stand with the fake Henry Ford quote. Customers will buy your product if they see it as the best choice. Beyond that, they can't answer too many of your complex business questions, and putting your decisions in the hands of your customers is generally a terrible idea.

Business gurus with years of experience don't know what's best for your business. Quite often, you don't know what's best for your business (otherwise why would you be tempted to ask customers). There is very little chance that a casual consumer of your product would know any better. In fact, this motto is so problematic now that customers have become so powerful that they think they can run businesses. But customers don't understand the risks and what's on the line. Sometimes you have to make people unhappy to save your business. Sometimes you have to choose the side of your staff over your customers because it's easier to get more customers than it is to get more great staff. Sometimes, as Henry Ford apparently claimed, customers don't know what they want.

One quote, which I know is correct, is this gem from Steve Jobs:

> *"It's really hard to design products by focus groups. A lot of times, people don't know what they want until you show it to them."* Steve Jobs

The Henry Ford quote might be bullshit, but this one isn't. Entrepreneurs are visionaries. They have to see a future situation where things are different than the current situation. They have to understand their products and their business better than anyone. Customers are not entrepreneurs. They offer one perspective: a glimpse on how you are currently servicing demand. But customers aren't visionaries, they don't think about the future. They think about solving their immediate problem.

You cannot delegate your job to customers. It's on you. It's your job to work out what people want now and in the future—and factor in your competition, the market, regulation, and a million other variables in defining a course of action, such as to work out what staff you need, what locations you need to operate in, what technologies to use, what causes you are going to support, what products you will offer, what products you will withdraw, what policies to put in place, and the list goes on and on. Customers don't care about half of that stuff, and with the stuff they do care about, they are just as likely to be angry at you for making the right, tough decision.

I am as big an advocate as you will ever get for giving great customer service. It remains one of the earliest, easiest, and most effective ways to differentiate a business to this day. But your service offering is always on your terms. It's *your* business, not your customer's business.

Do not delegate your entrepreneurial responsibilities to your customers. A good business has a customer that is happy. It doesn't mean they are always right.

VALIDATION IS A MYTH

In recent years, validation has entered into the entrepreneurial discussion as the ultimate cop-out. The lean startup movement created a group of entrepreneurs who were so set on validating their idea that they forgot to be entrepreneurs.

We tried to make entrepreneurs into scientists, but there was one problem: Entrepreneurs are not scientists.

Scientists get funding from governments to run experiments. The experiments are costly. If they fail, they learn something; if they succeed, they learn something. When they run out of funding, they seek more and do it all again. Failure and success are the same things to a scientist. The scientist is only motivated by learning more about whether their hypothesis is right or wrong, so failure or success in any given experiment will take them closer to that goal.

For most people, entrepreneurship is not like that. There isn't an endless string of generous donors looking to throw money at experiments, so most entrepreneurs are drastically underfunded. When you use your limited resources to start randomly testing certain hypotheses, you are going to run out of money very quickly.

But there's a bigger problem. Entrepreneurs are very rarely working on unique problems, and this is where the validation idea falls down.

Because I wrote a book about startups, and I have a group filled with entrepreneurs trying to figure it all out, I get to see a lot of examples of this. I'm constantly bombarded by messages and posts from people who are trying to validate X.

The funny thing is that everything they try to validate has already been validated by others.

I'll hear things like, "I currently have a marketplace for cleaners; I need to validate whether people will pay to get their place cleaned by a third party." There's no need to do that because there's plenty of cleaning marketplaces already, so consider it validated and get back to work, please.

Or, "I started a service for helping people create nicer graphics for their website, so I need to validate whether people will pay for it." Let me stop you there. There is no need to do that because graphic designers have been in existence for hundreds of years.

Or, "I have a software tool that automatically schedules people's social media, so I need to validate whether people want their social media automated and how much they will pay for that." No, you don't. Hootsuite has had a quarter of a billion dollars in funding by very smart investors to solve that exact same problem. Countless other companies like HubSpot and Buffer have built multiple eight-figure and nine-figure businesses doing that exact same thing. How much validation do you need?

They have been inspired by one-off success stories of MVPs like DropBox that have skewed their perception of how this stuff works. But these are increasingly rare cases, and the thousands of other companies who also set out to build MVPs and "validate" their ideas are dead and gone.

Most entrepreneurs are underfunded, and they can't go on constantly attempting to validate their ideas. But fortunately for them, in most cases, they don't have to.

Think of the types of questions that some of the biggest and most impactful startups would have had to ponder to get where they are.

Tesla - Will people buy a car that costs the same as a Nissan Pulsar, that is faster than a Porsche, and costs virtually $0 to run? Yeah, I think so.

AirBnB - If people could easily book accommodation on their phones in private places that were much bigger and more interesting than hotels and pay less, would they? Of course, we know they would.

Uber - If people didn't need to wait up to three hours, risk getting assaulted, get ripped off, and travel in a smelly car home, and instead they could press a button on their phone, get a friendly person to turn up within minutes in a nice car and be driven home for 40% of the price, would they? I don't need to answer that.

Validation has become the ultimate excuse for the modern entrepreneur. Meanwhile, the people who have really disrupted industries and built massive recognizable brands have instead focused on the task at hand for most entrepreneurs, which is to sell their idea and put it into action. They don't need validation; they don't need permission; they just need to get to work.

For most entrepreneurial stories, the mystery in the equation is not whether or not it's a good idea. Most of the problems we are all working on are generally proven ideas. The part that isn't proven is whether or not we can bring them to life. Whether we can sell the idea to investors or to customers. Whether we can market the idea and make it appealing enough for people to get on board. Whether we are the ones to finally change people's behaviours. We are only ever validating ourselves.

Your idea is probably sound. To be honest, it's probably already been done. The question is whether *you* can turn this into a business. And you don't do it by acting like a passive scientist, meddling with random experiments without a care for pass or fail. You do it by getting to work. By being an entrepreneur.

And look, you might not have it in you. You might have to go work for someone who does.

Not everyone can be an entrepreneur.

REDUCE YOUR PRICES

As a new entrepreneur, you will be bombarded with a raft of generic business truth's that the experts will drum into you to help you succeed. One of my all time favourites is "increase your prices."

Over the years, I've seen this advice everywhere you could imagine: in books, at live events, in startup incubators, at local co-working spaces, in online forums, live from stage, in paid info products, in free ebooks—it's almost a universally accepted business truth among online entrepreneurs in particular.

I bought into this advice early on in my career as an entrepreneur when I had my agency. I tried to do larger web projects, bring out monthly higher-priced services, and sell higher-ticket memberships. They all failed, and it was only when I aggressively sought to cut prices that my fortunes turned.

What I noticed about everyone telling me to increase prices was that they were almost always consultants of some kind: web agency owners, sales consultants, project managers, or people who had built up six-figure consultancies and gone on to be seen as experts because of that. Most of these guys were natural salespeople and could probably just as easily sell a $500 website as they could a $50,000 website.

The problem was that I didn't fit into this mold. Not only was I an average sales person and didn't want to market my business in that way, I also really had no desire to start or build a six-figure consultancy.

I started looking a bit broader for inspiration. I moved away from the local consultants and the expert online marketers and looked to the startup world to fill the void. I began by listening to *This Week in Startups* and other similar podcasts, and to my surprise, the advice was very different.

Most of the founders and the startup stories on *This Week In Startups* were looking to reduce prices. The host, Jason Calacanis, interviewed and talked about heavily funded startups, successful investors, and entrepreneurs who'd built seven, eight, nine, and ten-figure businesses. There were no local consultants in sight, and I didn't once hear about the idea of increasing prices to build your business.

In fact, it was the opposite.

I heard about Amazon operating for over 20 years without making a profit. I heard about Uber's goal of drastically improving the experience of being moved around, while also reducing the cost by 40%. I heard about AirBnB's idea of making it much easier to find good quality accommodation, all the while reducing the price significantly.

I heard about Elon Musk's dream of building a $35,000 car that would be faster than a Porsche and would be virtually free to run.

The list goes on and on. I noticed something about this group of entrepreneurs. They weren't motivated by making a short-term profit and building a nice comfortable business. These guys were disrupting gigantic industries. They were looking for massive product improvements and huge price reductions.

I realized two things hearing these stories:

1. The best entrepreneurs who are building the most exciting businesses right now, are not selling info products and not offering coaching services. I decided to learn from what people do, chase the stories of what people are working on, and avoid anyone who put themselves out there as an expert, especially those doing so by selling information products and memberships.

2. These entrepreneurs were truly innovating. When you innovate, prices come down; they don't go up.

I've heard "experts" say things like, "Don't reduce costs because you can only reduce them so far. Instead, increase your prices!"

They don't realize that you can also only increase your prices so far. Competition will always arise, and if your only means of innovating is increasing your prices, the competition will beat you.

But the "increase prices" option is far more damaging because it's dangled in front of naive entrepreneurs as an easy fix to a complex problem. Once the fix is in place, they no longer have to worry about the problem. But if your goal is ultimately to reduce prices through innovation, you can't ever stop thinking about it.

Innovation is at the core of entrepreneurship. I believe entrepreneurs are somewhere smack in the middle of salespeople and inventors. Salespeople will always want to make more money but at the expense of innovation. Inventors will always want to create more innovations, but for the most part, they are broke.

Entrepreneurs are in the middle. If your idea is to make a world-changing invention, and you have no plan for making money from it, then you aren't an entrepreneur. On the flip side, if your plan is to continue to increase your prices and have no innovative ideas, then you aren't an entrepreneur.

I challenge you to create a better product, a better experience, a better brand, a better offer—at a lower price. That's entrepreneurship.

YOUR DESIGN SUCKS
AND THAT MATTERS

Not a day goes by without me seeing a post on Facebook with a founder presenting three versions of their logo and asking for an opinion on which one is best.

I have learned to ignore 90% of them, but when I do feel the need to reply, my response is always the same:

1. Every design you have listed is terrible.

2. Why would you ask your friends, who know nothing about design, to give you advice on design? You might as well ask

them for a checkup and some legal advice while you're at it.

3. Any process that results in you showing off three versions of a logo to your friends is fundamentally flawed.

4. It really doesn't matter what I say because obviously, you know nothing about design and neither does your designer, so in the end, it will be up to you two, and it will be a terrible result.

I'm a design tragic. I've never really been able to design things well myself, but like most people, I like to think I've got a good eye for design.

The problem is, most people don't have a good eye for design. The design of their logos and websites proves that, and their constant need for external validation confirms it.

As Jason Calacanis, the host of *This Week in Startups*, said in 2012, we live in the age of excellence. You can't fake it anymore. Product matters, service matters, reviews matter, design matters, it all matters. No one will admit it, and no customer will ever tell you they signed up because of your design, but they did. They subconsciously compare your execution of the solution to their problem and the major competitors' execution, and they choose the best.

Good entrepreneurs are almost universally design-driven. Look at the way Steve Jobs executed on his vision for Apple and worked relentlessly with Jony Ive on the design of their products. Look at the key hires made by Elon Musk at Tesla and the amount of thought and design brilliance that goes into his cars, his rockets, his tunnel concepts, even his prototype space suits. No one is going into space on Elon's watch without looking good!

The best startups in the world hire world-class designers first. They even give up substantial equity to designers and quite often have a designer on the founding team.

Yet, we still have countless entrepreneurs trying to solve design problems by desperately posting three concepts on Facebook.

Most entrepreneurs don't value design. Here are some of the things I've seen that demonstrate their lack of value for the design field. If you see yourself doing these, then you know which type of entrepreneur you are. These also represent an opportunity for anyone who wants to stand out from the crowd of entrepreneurs who don't value design and join the best entrepreneurs who value it before everything else.

YOU DON'T KNOW WHAT GOOD DESIGN LOOKS LIKE

It's going to be impossible to put together a good brand or website for your company if you have no idea what good design looks like. Most people look at their friends' businesses to get design inspiration. That's a terrible idea. Your friends know nothing about design either.

I suggest looking at the world's best startups. Analyze their name, their logo, their images, their fonts, the way they interact with customers, the words they use—everything—in fine detail.

Follow trends outside your direct niche. Listen to interviews with great designers. Look through AngelList to find how the top startups are designing their sites. Learn to love architecture and analyze your favorite physical products.

You will quickly learn that your friend's website isn't as great as you thought. You'll also learn that simple design is much more complex than you originally thought. Poor designers add in elements so you have everything you could ever need, and the result is something that looks terrible and feels clunky. Great designers take most things away, so you are left with something that does one thing well and feels elegant.

Have you noticed that the whole world complains every time a new Apple product comes out missing some feature? They complained when they made a keyboard without a back button. They complained when they brought out the MacBook Air with no CD drive. They complained when they brought out the MacBook with no USB drive. They complained when they brought out the iPhone without support for Flash. They complained when they brought out newer iPhone models without headphone jacks. They were laughed at when they brought out earphones with no cords!

But like Robbie Williams says, "You can't argue with popularity. Well, you could, but you'd be wrong!"

All of these products went on to be revolutionary products that culminated in Apple becoming the most valuable company on earth. That's because Apple has a culture of design started by a founder obsessed with design, and they hire the world's best designers because they all want to work for Apple. And the customers who complained didn't get it because they don't get design.

They can't see the value that delivering less can bring if it's executed well.

THEY HIRE CHEAP DESIGNERS

If you are starting out and you don't want to spend thousands on a logo, my guess is you are going to rush to a design competition site. What you may not realize is that world-class designers are in huge demand. They don't submit logos to marketplace sites on the off chance they will land a $200 payday. Good designers have an endless list of people who will pay them $5,000 or $10,000 for a logo. The world's best designers have an endless list of people who will pay them a multiple six-figure salary and give up a decent chunk of equity in their company to have them on board.

There are really only two ways to avoid this trap. You can pay for a good or a great designer, or if you have a smaller unfunded project, you can avoid custom design altogether. Most designers can not design a brand or a website as well as the best themes available. Entrepreneurs are better off using a well-designed premium theme and having no logo than they would using a poor design.

Once you are more established, you can spend up on your own unique, world-class brand. Just skip the bit in the middle where you hire a crappy designer to design you an even crappier brand.

THEY LISTEN TO THE WRONG PEOPLE

If you are in the group of entrepreneurs who post their design ideas on Facebook for review, please stop. You wouldn't go to Facebook if you were looking for a constipation cure. You wouldn't ask Facebook to help with your indecent exposure defence plan. There are experts for these things, and you value those experts because you believe the thing is important.

If you believe design is important, you consult the experts.

Another thing I see a lot is getting your developer to do design. Developers are developers, designers are designers. A deviner is a developer who is also a designer. They are like a unicorn or a lawyer who is also a good person. I'm sure they exist; I've just never seen one.

The bottom line is that people who don't understand design should not be making your design choices.

THE PROCESS WAS FLAWED OR NONEXISTENT

Most bad design stems from a bad design process that comes from a designer who lacks confidence. A confident designer will not get a one-page brief from you and give you three concepts and encourage you to share it among your friends and customers for their opinion.

It's not important for you to get feedback from your customers on your design. It's not important to split test your design. Design cannot be quantified.

A good design process will work in reverse. The designer should have a deep understanding of your business and your customers based on their discovery process. They should know what you stand for and what shapes, patterns, materials and textures you like. They should know what you care about, what motivates your staff, and what the company stands for. They should have used your product and know it well. They should know your history and your origins and your vision. But they also should know your limitations. Bad clients are one of the biggest reasons for bad design. Once they know all of this, they will be in a place to start thinking about how to design for you.

But they shouldn't be doing this in isolation. You should know them, too. You should know what tools they use, what inspires them. You should know design and architecture and web design. You should have favorite companies and favourite products and favourite shapes. You should intimately know your competitors and be able to think and feel like them when they make purchasing decisions. You should have a vision yourself, and you shouldn't let yourself be pushed around by a designer who has their own agenda. Most importantly, you should understand the commercial realities within which this design sits. You shouldn't let designers get carried away with creativity. It's your business, it's your product, and the brand is everything you stand for. Don't delegate it.

If this sounds like some kind of brutally aggressive war, maybe it is. Sometimes, that's how design works.

Sometimes, you will flow with your designer, and sometimes, you will fight with your designer. Design can be a very stressful process. Or it can be a magical process where it all flows perfectly well. Or 90% of it could be smooth sailing and the last 10% could be pure hell. Don't stop before the hell. It's not always easy. We aren't dealing with lines and dots here, we are dealing with curves.

A good design process will be 80% digging and 20% designing. A process that involves competition sites or cheap designers who insist on giving you three shitty concepts to share with your non-designer friends has failed before it's begun.

YOU TRIED TO BE CREATIVE

Oh, no, here we go. You've chosen a nice theme and just want to make a few tweaks to it. Or worse, you've dug out the tools and tried to throw your own logo together.

Please, please, please don't do that. Show some more respect to the design profession and get the pros to do it.

I'm a strong believer that everyone is creative. But I also value skills, and the best designers have spent years living a life that revolves around design. It's not just the skills using their hands or using the software; it's everything else. It's their appreciation for design in other fields and their experience working on other projects. It's their living and breathing design all day every day for their whole lives.

Again, it doesn't mean they know everything about your business and can nail your design without your input. But it does mean they have earned your respect in their profession.

Design is not about being creative.

Design is complex.

It doesn't happen by chance, and it's not a skill you can acquire from an ebook. Respect the design profession because you ain't got this.

In summary, don't create a product or branding material without giving a lot of thought to design. It's important, and it's a core entrepreneurial skill in the age of excellence.

INVESTORS ARE NOT EVIL

Recently, I came across yet another Facebook post where someone was tossing up whether or not to get an investor for their business. Of course, the comments are a constant barrage of negativity: "Don't do it!" "You don't need it." "Bootstrap all the way."

Maybe it's the circles I'm in, but I regularly come across this attitude. I'm all for people sharing their opinions online, but I wonder how much of this opinion comes from ignorance?

Us bootstrapped crowd of entrepreneurs look up to the modern titans of entrepreneurship and the big brands of our day (who pretty much all had external funding), but somehow we are not okay with the idea of investors?

I've been a big fan and advocate of bootstrapping over the years and was lucky enough to bootstrap a million-dollar business that was sold to a multi-billion-dollar business, but I still don't think that investors are evil and bootstrapping is the only way. I'd be an idiot if I thought that. While I was building my million-dollar business, there were entrepreneurs building businesses that were doing $10m in revenue, $100m in revenue, and yes, billions in revenue! The vast majority of these businesses had investors. Without them, they would not exist, or at least would not be anywhere near their level of success.

Growth hacking is a hot topic right now, and it's lead to every startup entrepreneur and his dog thinking they can shortcut building large companies. But the reality is that growth is extremely expensive. Disruption isn't just a buzzword. Disruption often requires aggressively taking down existing companies with lower priced and more efficient methods. This comes at a price and most often the price is paid for by investors.

By definition, it's impossible to be hugely profitable and be a disruptive innovator. After all, if you are that profitable, it just leaves a lot of room for other people to come in and disrupt you.

Normally, building a big, high-growth, and significant company means being unprofitable for an uncomfortable amount of time.

I remember when I was first introduced to circles of online marketers and solopreneurs, and Amazon was talked about as the laughing stock of business. They had lost money for twenty years straight. Why do that when you can make a profit from day one?

The answer is obvious in hindsight. You don't become the richest person on earth by building a small, yet profitable business.

I made my way through that journey and now find myself in a company (Black Hops Brewing) with a lot of investors. In fact, we have over thirty, and have embarked on an equity crowdfunding round that could increase that number into the hundreds if not thousands.

I used to be quite "anti-investor" as well, but to be honest, I had no idea how you would even get investors. No one had ever expressed interest in investing in any of my companies before. Our current investors have come about through pure necessity. We had a few hundred thousand dollars to put into our business, but it costs multiple millions to make it happen. Without investors, we would not exist.

Black Hops is a lot bigger and more valuable than anything I've done before. Of course, I don't own 100% of it, but my argument has always been the same. I gave up 50% of WP Curve because I thought 50% of $1,000,000 was better than 100% of $100,000. And it's the same with Black Hops.

We can only get so far ourselves, so we give up a decent chunk of equity to try to achieve something much bigger, and ultimately, we own a smaller, but more valuable stake.

I think a lot of the disdain for investors comes from a basic assumption about business that is wrong. The assumption is that if you have a good business, it will throw off enough cash for profits and enough profits to reward the founders. If the business doesn't do that, then the business just isn't good enough, and investors will only make it worse.

If you think this way, let me ask you this: Can you name one brand that you love, that has not at some point had outside funding.

And before you say "Basecamp," you might be interested in knowing that the legends of boot-strapping actually did sell a percentage of their company to an outside investor. And, as fate would have it, that investor was the founder of Amazon, Jeff Bezos, the richest man on earth.

The truth is that in most cases, focusing 100% on short-term profit will compromise other things. Things that will ultimately lead to more value.

Starting the sort of business that can be profitable right from the outset is probably a sign that you are creating the sort of business that can never be that valuable. Freelancing is an easy way to make a profit, but you can never get investors and never sell the business because the business is not worth anything.

If you want to start the kind of business that ultimately has other people wanting to own it, it probably doesn't start with a whole lot of profit.

Investors are not the answer for every business. I think most of the people I see debating whether or not they need investors have the sort of business that investors would never invest in anyway. It's a philosophical debate with no real consequences. They are ignorantly building a small lifestyle business that actually isn't valuable. If you have a business that attracts outside investment, it's probably not a bad sign.

Getting investors means selling some of your business. If you can't sell some of your business, then what is it really worth?

No one is going to have their business forever, so the ultimate goal of any business should be to sell at some point. If you choose not to look that far into the future, then that's fine. But if you do want to look to the future and consider who might buy your business, then is it such a bad idea to sell some of it now?

For some businesses and some situations, you need outside money. The fact that someone wants to put money into your business and own some of it is a good sign. It means you are creating something valuable. Maybe you have a vision that stretches more than five minutes into the future, and you have been able to sell that vision to someone else. This is not a bad thing.

If you are a bootstrapped founder, don't get too distracted by other bootstrapped founders telling you how to do things. It's okay to have ambitions bigger than creating a reasonable income for yourself. It's okay to take much bigger risks, and it's okay to build a business that requires you to get other people's money to do it—if that's what the business needs.

DON'T HAVE HEROES

You don't have to look too far these days to come across entire generations of people who have been devastated after learning that the person they grew up adoring is not who they thought.

There's a saying: Never meet your heroes. And it exists because if you spend any amount of time worshipping someone who you have never met and really know nothing about, it's probably not going to end well.

Yet, it's completely accepted and considered normal to have heroes. I think that's weird. I've even been considered somewhat of a mentor to other people in business at times, and it's a position

I've never been comfortable with. For about ten years, I've been pretty outspoken on various business topics, and over the years, I've put out a lot of content. For the first three or four years, it all went unnoticed. I wrote hundreds and hundreds of blog posts from 2009 to 2012, and only one or two posts got any traction at all.

From 2013 onward, when WP Curve took off, things started to change. I had some success in business, and then all of a sudden everyone wanted to hear from me. I kept putting out more or less the same sort of content, and things got on a roll. I wrote a book, *The 7 Day Startup* that sold tens of thousands of copies, and I then wrote a second book, a third book, and a fourth book. I was regularly asked to speak at events and appeared on hundreds of podcasts, including some pretty big business ones like *Mixergy* and *Smart Passive Income* with Pat Flynn.

That one story about me starting that business and growing it took hold, and suddenly, I was a business guru. When I went to events, I met so many people who looked up to me and wanted me to figure out their business problems. I actually felt bad for them because I couldn't help them. I felt lucky to have been able to figure out one out of hundreds of my own business problems, and there was no way I was going to be able to figure out theirs. I'm sure a lot of people who met me were probably disappointed, which begs the question of why would they look up to me in the first place, and did that actually serve them?

We've all felt this scenario before. We see something from the outside one way, and once inside, we see it in a whole new light.

To me, anything that takes you further away from being an entrepreneur isn't worth indulging in. As an entrepreneur, it's your job to figure out your own problems and if you are lucky enough to have people on the inside with you, work on it with them.

I truly believe that if I have an issue with my brewery business, my co-founders, Eddie and

Govs, would be able to help me more than Elon Musk would. I think this is a good way to think. It's taking ultimate responsibility yourself and not hoping some guru will be able to dig you out of your hole.

FAILURE IS NOT THE GOAL

I built a career and an amazing lifestyle off the back of telling my failure story. In 2012, after 6 years of entrepreneurship, I was broke. I'd lost $80,000 the previous year, 100% of my net worth (if you exclude superannuation, which was almost non-existent anyway), and I was back to looking for a job. I'd been forced to sell my house, having not been able to afford it, and I'd sold my previous business, having not being able to make anything of it.

I was diagnosed with depression and anxiety, and I was on medication for ADHD. I was a new parent and in a thirteen-year relationship that would ultimately end in divorce not long after.

I'd started sharing income reports online because I liked the idea. I like to joke now that in 2012 my posts were just reports because there was no income.

I can still remember the feeling. I worried what my kids—who were getting to the age where they were asking, "What does Dad do for work"—were going to think of me. I didn't know who I was. I'd spent six years telling my friends and family that I was an entrepreneur, so why the fuck was I looking for jobs?

Sorry for the feels, but when you tell a story about failure, you have to talk about how you feel. You can't just give facts, it's feelings that really draws people in.

That's the problem with failure. It's compelling. And despite being a person who's built their current existence off the back of a failure story, I worry that it's become far too cool.

When I decided to write this book, I put a call out on my 7 Day Startup Facebook Group for stories about entrepreneurs who had hustled hard to achieve something. I had a message from one person saying, "You should check out Faras Idham. He's a local entrepreneur who hustled really hard to build his local transport startup, which ultimately crashed and burned." I said that was not exactly what I was looking for, so she suggested another one. What about "Jane O'Brien, who worked her arse off, raised a ton of money, launched a fitness range that almost became a household name, but ultimately failed and lost all of the investors' money?"

"I'm sorry," I said. "I have to be honest; I'm not really after failure stories, I'm after success stories." She couldn't think of any more examples of entrepreneurs.

I understand the role of failure, and I myself have written about how it can be a good thing. But I'm nervous that today's entrepreneur has been bombarded so much with failure stories that they've forgotten that failure is actually not the goal.

Failure is seen as a right of passage. It's a must-have in every success story. There has to be a rock bottom because it helps people relate. Anyone who is currently at that rock bottom can relate to being at rock bottom.

It's cool for people like J.K. Rowling to be at rock bottom and come back to become the world's richest and most successful and well-known author. It's a great story, so we celebrate it.

But what of the people who stay at rock bottom? What about the people who enjoy being at rock bottom? What if all of these failure stories are breeding a group of entrepreneurs who are so obsessed with failure that they actually forget the point? Which, of course, is to succeed, not to fail.

The biggest problem I have with failure is the same problem I have with entrepreneurial advice in general. And that is the assumption that the entrepreneur actually knows the reason for success or failure.

With failure, it's well accepted that you can learn from it and move forward. But in my experience, sometimes things just don't work. In fact, most of the time things don't work. You can either analyze the shit out of it, or even worse, actually embrace it and become it, or you can just accept it didn't work and move on—ideally to success (eventually). If you focus too much on the failure, your attention is diverted from the real goal, which is, of course, not to fail.

The same issue exists with success. Sometimes, you have amazing and extremely fortunate timing. It doesn't come down to a specific tactic you can emulate, it's just a (dare I say it) lucky sequence of events.

For me, my rock bottom failure moment led to an extremely fortunate and unexpected series of events. I didn't get any of the jobs I was looking at. I started a WordPress support business in seven days. Two years later, it was a million dollar business. Soon after, I had a meeting with a multinational corporation who would ultimately buy the business. That meeting was on the exact day we opened our brewery, which in the two-plus years since has become a multi-million dollar business, far more valuable than the last one. My story of starting a business in seven days led me to write five books and having a virtually passive six-figure annual income for the last three years just for my personal brand alone.

It's a great story; you couldn't make this shit up. But I always try to remind myself that the failure is not the story. Failure is fucked. I wouldn't wish it upon any entrepreneur, and I'm not convinced we should be glorifying it.

The failure is what gets people into the story, but what we are really after is the success. It's useful not to forget that.

Don't get distracted by failure porn.

Don't be afraid to celebrate success.

Failure is not the goal.

Success is the goal.

GOOD BUSINESS IS EASY

It's one of the ruthless aspects of business. When things are going well, they are going very well. When they aren't—well, they aren't.

Being part of a business that constantly fails is tough. You feel like you are doing great work. You probably are. But no matter what you do, you can't move the needle. You improve your product, you upskill yourself, you talk to your customers, read books, change pricing—you name it. But success eludes you.

On the other hand, when things are on a roll, no matter how many mistakes you make, things keep going in the right direction. You screw up a few jobs, miss a few deals, waste time on the wrong things, and get distracted, but things still keep powering on.

I've experienced both situations regularly in my life as an entrepreneur, often both at the same time. This last year I've seen my personal brand dissipate to almost nothing. My online community was going backward, so I cancelled it. I wrote no new books and existing book sales went down significantly. All the while, my main business, Black Hops, has been exploding, and I have had the best business year of my life.

Deciding to move away from my personal brand wasn't exactly easy. There was a constant barrage of social media posts and external validation saying I should keep it up. But the reality was that Black Hops was a freight train and was leaving the station. My personal brand was dying off. I chose to focus on what had momentum, and I left behind something that was slowing down.

Before I wrote my very first book, *The 7 Day Startup*, I sat down to write some words for a potential book to be called *Momentum*. I never did write the book, but I haven't changed my thinking on the point. Momentum is the most powerful force in business. So much failure can be put down to working on something that has no momentum. So much success can be put down to just being there in a situation where something has momentum.

The "work hard" ethic isn't always that helpful. Sometimes it's not that hard. And if it is really hard, that could be a bad sign.

Don't expect things to be hard. Don't glorify things being hard. Instead, keep your eye out for easy. Momentum can work a hell of a lot harder than you can. The goal should be to find a place where your business is moving forward on its own, and you are just there making sure nothing stops that momentum.

NEVER BUILD TO SELL BUT ALWAYS BUILD SOMETHING SALEABLE

I n my current industry of craft beer brewing, it's very common for successful companies to be sold to big players. Normally, when that happens, there's an uproar in the craft beer groups about "selling out," and the companies take a hit on sales (at least in the short term).

Because of that, this is one of the questions we are asked all the time. "What's the end game?" "Is the plan to sell the business?" We get asked this from customers, fans, journalists, staff, and existing and potential investors.

I've been asked this more times as an entrepreneur than I can remember. Every time I hear it, I think, *Who actually builds a business for the sole purpose of selling it?* Maybe it is a thought, but I can't think of anyone I know who has ever done this. People who ask that question are usually ignorant of the way things normally work in entrepreneurship. Normally, a business owner passionately builds a business, and if things go well, it takes off. At some point down the track, the possibility of selling comes up because of how well they've done at pouring their blood and sweat into their creation. Sometimes, they are presented with an offer they can't refuse. Sometimes, they are just ready to move on to something new. I'd say most of the time they just can't afford to fund its growth, so selling becomes the only viable option. But it was never planned. If it were planned, particularly in the story-driven businesses I build, people would see through it from the start. The plan should always be to build a great business and create value for your customers.

That said, you'd have to be crazy to start a business and never once consider the possibility of one day selling it. It's much like buying a house. It wouldn't be smart to buy a quirky house in an average neighbourhood just because you thought it was cool without considering whether the house would go up in value. Sure, you may not have plans to sell, and you may think you will never sell, but even so, it's a huge investment, so you'd want it to be more valuable in the future than it is now.

There's no bigger investment than starting a business. Even if you don't pour millions of dollars into it in the form of startup capital, or reduced wages, you'll never get back your time. And as Felix Dennis says, "We're wealthier in this moment than we'll ever be in the future" because the currency of the highest value is time. Your business will consume years of your life that you'll never get back, so make sure it's worth something when you're finished. It won't be worth anything if you treat it like a commodity that you can buy or sell.

I always like to have a handle on how much my business might be worth. I wouldn't recommend this to all entrepreneurs, but one way you can do it is to raise money. In other words, sell part of it to investors. Entrepreneurs and business valuation experts are not good at determining the value of new companies, but if an investor is willing to invest at a certain valuation, then you know it's worth something.

Even if you don't decide to raise money, don't discount the importance of having some idea what your brand is ultimately worth. Look at other investment rounds, read up on exits, learn to critically compare what you are building to other companies with proven valuations. A business is more than just a way to create a nice wage for yourself. A business should one day become a valuable brand. You may think you will never sell. Not true. Everything is sold eventually in one way or another. You might as well understand the value now so you don't spend years building something worthless.

Most entrepreneurs vastly overestimate the value of their business. If you stop working and your business stops running, it's not worth much at all. It's very difficult to build something that can run well under new ownership.

For me, I hope we never sell Black Hops unless we decide we no longer want to do the work. But regardless, from before we started, my focus had been to build something valuable. And along the way, I've stayed on top of how much it might be worth.

DON'T NICHE DOWN

When you start your business, everyone will tell you to find a small group of people to sell to. In other words, find a niche of specific buyers that you can serve well. This is almost a universally accepted truth in the circles I travel in.

Years ago, I was quite active in the online marketing/internet marketing industry. Out of all the tried and true pieces of business advice given to me over those years, I had this "niche down" message drummed into me more than anything else. Those words were so common it became painful. Literally. It got as extreme as "niche down until it hurts, and then niche down some more."

I never agreed at the time, and I don't agree now. I think all valuable companies serve large markets and getting from small to large doesn't mean you have to niche down. In fact, niching down will often make it harder to get from small to large.

The accepted wisdom is that it makes sense to start small, build a loyal customer base, and then naturally outgrow that small market and go after a bigger one.

For me, this advice causes more problems than it helps. I see a lot of entrepreneurs with successful niche businesses, but they've hit a ceiling and lost momentum. It impacts your productivity, your growth, and your motivation, and you start second-guessing your strategy. Most of these businesses stagnate at best, but more often than not fail because the founder gets bored and unhappy and moves on.

One of my online heroes once said that "underwater samurai sword training" was a big enough niche.

It's funny these days when I look back at all the people around then and their companies and where they are at now. In particular, how many of them were able to grow beyond where they were, and how many are either still there or not in business at all. There are only a handful of entrepreneurs I can think of who escaped that circle. One started a software business in a broad market segment and was able to build it into a $10MM+ annual business. Another started a physical goods business that became worth tens of millions of dollars.

Most of the others are still there, chasing niches, chasing small opportunities, and all the while selling products to educate other entrepreneurs to do the same thing. They are still selling the "niche down" message to other new entrepreneurs who are building shitty niche businesses with just enough cash flow to prop up their mentors' niche info-product business.

If you think about most of the entrepreneurs who have created truly impactful businesses, they didn't create a niche business. They may have started out small, and they may have started with only a few customers, but ultimately, they were building something that could potentially have millions of customers.

Creating something for a broad market is risky, but that's what entrepreneurship is. Attempting to avoid risk by targeting small niches only creates the ultimate long-term risk—you won't succeed in doing anything significant.

The easiest path to having a business serving a large market is to start a business serving a large market. When I say easy, I mean you will probably fail, probably go through periods of extreme stress and borderline depression, and maybe one day figure it out. But that path, the path of an entrepreneur, is a more likely path than creating a business to serve a small niche.

With my WordPress business, it served a huge market from day one. When we started, there was a market of 70 million websites running WordPress in every country, in every timezone, no matter what kind of business.

For us, it meant:

- Zero changes in strategy from day one. Our first customer signed up for a monthly WordPress support subscription, so did our thousandth customer.

- We had clear targets and goals with no expectation of our growth letting up or having to pivot once we hit a ceiling.

- We had immediate referability because everyone knows someone with a website running WordPress.

- We were immediately on the WordPress radar, being featured in big sites virtually from day one. It's very hard to get press and attention for businesses that serve niches, other than in the niche itself.

- We were able to explain our business to people easily, and they have been able to pass it on.

- We had a better return on our content marketing because a huge percentage of the audience of any site we end up on uses WordPress.

With my brewery, Black Hops, it's not all that different. Craft beer is a small segment of the market in Australia, but it's hardly a niche. The overall beer market is billions of dollars just in Australia. For craft beer specifically, it's still a huge market with hundreds of millions of dollars just in our region, and there are only a handful of breweries.

This is very helpful. There are all sorts of challenges we have in business, but one thing we don't have to worry about is hitting some kind of ceiling with demand. If we can keep making great beers, there will be plenty of demand for those beers. Our growth hasn't let up since the beginning. Our first month, we turned over $26,000 in revenue. Over two years later, we turned over $342,000 in our latest month.

The last thing you want to do as a business is to lose momentum. My good friend and serial entrepreneur, Sam, said to me recently, "Once momentum goes, it's a very hard thing to get back."

Momentum is the most powerful force in business, and when you choose to start serving a small niche and hope to outgrow it later, you plan on compromising your momentum at some stage.

Don't be afraid to enter into a large market. Be careful making rules for your business that will get in the way of momentum.

UNTARGET YOUR MARKETING

On March 1, 1998, I tentatively stepped through the entrance to Queensland University of Technology for my first day of a business degree majoring in marketing. My first semester would be rough with two fails and a conceded pass out of four subjects. The conceded pass concept was a great one. It meant that as long as you weren't majoring in the subject, a fail would count as a pass. It was like if you were smart enough, you could still pass if you failed. My problem was that my conceded pass was in marketing.

Lucky, I was smart, and it was an easy fix. I changed to Human Resources and never took another marketing subject.

But I do remember a few things from that first course. I remember this idea of having an avatar, which is defining a person to whom your business and marketing is aimed at. Give them a name, dig into what they like and don't like, how they think, what words they use, etc.

In 2006, after a short and unsuccessful career in human resources, I started my own business building websites and found myself back in the marketing game. Once again, I consistently came across this customer avatar idea.

Like niching down, I heard this so often that I tried it for myself over many years. But like niching down, it didn't work for me. And what worked for me was the complete opposite.

In the early days, I would specifically think about the type of customer who would buy my websites. They have a small business. Their name is probably Jane. They watch *Shark Tank*, and they like coffee and yoga on Sunday mornings. But that didn't really help me. I tried to target my marketing toward small business forums and websites and refine my copy, etc. I had the whole avatar mapped out, yet nothing I did got any traction.

Over time, that changed. In 2009 I gave up on traditional marketing. I started a blog and started writing down my ideas. I wrote ideas about how to build better websites and also documented some of my journey in business. Over a few years, my writing started getting a bit of traction. Come 2012/2013, I started doing income reports for my Analytics Dashboard startup idea, a business that ultimately failed.

During that time, I was constantly told that there was no ROI in blogging, or as I liked to call it, content marketing. But I kept it up, mainly because nothing else worked, and I felt like I could do it reasonably well.

This would have had to have been some of the most un-targeted marketing imaginable. I was literally writing blog posts and pushing publish.

But I kept the reports going. People followed along with the story, and when I launched WP Curve, and it took off, the story got a lot more interesting. That same audience I'd built from those blog posts had come along with me all the way and were now signing up as customers to my WordPress support business. It worked amazingly well.

From then on, I've never done traditional marketing, I've only tried to build a brand and tell a story. My marketing has been very broad and for anyone who wanted to read it. Some people would read it and sign up and become a customer, but this was rare. Most people would see it, and that would be it. They might tell someone, they might share it, but mostly they would just read it and then move onto the next interesting piece of content. Over time, these people learned to trust me and the brands I was working on. Over the years, readers became advocates and even evangelists. Some became suppliers. Some became collaborators. Some became co-founders! Over time, the businesses found their customers by building a great brand.

There was nothing targeted about it. There was no avatar. But it worked far better than any targeted strategy I ever undertook.

TAKE OBSCENE RISKS

One of the big trends in recent entrepreneurship discussions is this idea that you can somehow mitigate the risks of entrepreneurship. The Lean Startup movement kicked this off by convincing everyone that you could simply create a series of small experiments, test them quickly, and move on, thereby negating any serious entrepreneurial risk.

But the years since have proven that, for the most part, this isn't the case. Startups are failing as fast and in as devastating fashion as they always have. We've learned that entrepreneurship can't really be whittled down into a simple A/B test. It's not simple, and it's not guaranteed. If it were, it would cease to be entrepreneurship, and it would become the mainstream path. What we are seeing is a little bit more entrepreneurialism creeping into the mainstream path. People renting out their house on AirBNB, people driving for Uber on the weekends; a small amount of hustle brings a small reward.

But this isn't really entrepreneurship. Entrepreneurship has the potential to bring huge rewards, but more likely, massive losses. If all you are doing is following a clear path with a tiny bit of hustle thrown in, you aren't being an entrepreneur. The potential to bring huge rewards is offset by the risk required to do so. Once things become less risky, the mainstream flood in, they become commoditized, and the huge potential reward goes away.

By definition, you cannot be an entrepreneur if you aren't prepared to take big risks.

One argument I often find myself having is with people who are stuck in project work and freelancing. In the best of cases, they are earning what they would earn if they had a job, but they get to "work from home" and "live on their own terms." I've even had some of them claim they don't like the term "entrepreneur" and don't identify with it.

They are giving up their legal rights as an employee (things like pay for hours worked, sick leave, long service leave, superannuation, etc.), dropping job security, and leaving all of their friends behind to pursue this dream of working for themselves. The risks are significant. They might not get enough work to earn minimum wage. They might work 16 hours a day and get paid less than they would working for someone else. They might have one client not pay them and render a whole month of work wasted. They might turn into a hermit working for themselves. They might scrape by for 20 years, and at the end realize they haven't been paying themselves Superannuation/401k and have nothing to show for it. They might do it for 30 years, and at the end, realize that they don't have anything of value to see as a result, just the money they earned during that time (which they probably invested back into the various businesses).

And what is the potential reward of taking all of this risk? Not a whole lot. There's not much potential to earn much more than they would working for someone else. They aren't building anything they could one day sell for millions of dollars. Sure, they get to work at home, but there are just as many negatives as positives that come with working from home. I would say there are more.

To me, it doesn't make sense. If you're going to take on the risks, then take the risks fully, and leave yourself open to some significant rewards.

I've taken some risks in my time as an entrepreneur that have felt very significant. Two weeks after getting the biggest promotion of my life in 2006, I left my cushy government job to start a business building websites. I had never built a website before and had no customers. A few years prior, I was desperate to take any job I could, and here I was walking away from one paying twice as much as my first job.

Toward the end of that journey, I bought another company that did something similar. I paid about $50,000, using money I borrowed. Either I was going to make this work, or I would be fucked and would have to sell my house to pay back the loan. It turned out I was fucked and had to sell my house, with tens of thousands of dollars worth of losses, to make back the difference.

After seven years of failing at that business, I offered to give half of it away to another two guys who would become my business partners. We couldn't come to terms, so that fell through, and I ended up selling it for about a year's worth of pay with no idea of what I'd do. That was in my early 30s, no longer owning any property, with two young kids, a marriage that was dissolving, and feeling like a complete failure as an entrepreneur. But the risks were far from over.

All of that money went into a product that was a dismal failure. A year later, I was two weeks away from running out of runway completely with nothing to my name. I sent a desperate email to my email list to start a WordPress support business (WP Curve). That idea started to take off, and a few months in, I decided I needed to staff it on the other side of the world. In that same week, I had a comment on one of my blog posts from an Aussie who had just moved to San Francisco. "Hey Dan, love these posts. Have you ever considered taking on a co-founder?"

After a few phone calls, I decided to give up virtually half of that business to someone I had never met before.

I would work with him for nine months before we finally met in person. We ended up building a million-dollar business together and selling it to GoDaddy two years later.

The risks didn't stop there. When two mates and I decided we wanted to open a brewery, I committed to putting in $100,000 to kick it off. I didn't have $100,000, so I had to back myself to make that money in the six months before opening to enable me to chip in to build the brewery. On top of that, we also had to raise $150,000 from other investors to open the doors. By this time, we'd already decided to do it and put orders in, so not going ahead wasn't an option.

This all happened before selling my previous business, so I didn't have cash lying around. Did I mention I was also going through a divorce at the time?

The risks didn't stop there. Two years later, our brewery hit capacity, and we decided we needed to build a much bigger brewery. We signed a lease that would cost us just under a million dollars over five years in a new factory. We had $0 in the bank and were losing money each month. I had two weeks to raise $2.5MM to fund the new brewery, all under the ASIC restrictions that dictated that we couldn't advertise the raise and we couldn't have more than 20 investors. I was able to raise $1.7MM, which was enough to order the equipment and give us hope that one day we could fill the factory and open the new location.

We lived to fight another day, but I still had six months to come up with the remaining $800,000. The project went over budget, so we were short over $1MM, and that was only the money required to open up. Once we opened, we'd be up for a huge amount of cash to ramp up production in the new facility. We spent six months talking to every major bank and a range of second, third, fourth, and god-knows-what tier lenders. We ran an equity crowdfunding campaign where we hoped we could raise $150,000 to $400,000 to help. I also looked into another investment raise and started talking to a few investors about a convertible note.

A month after our scheduled opening, we hadn't raised a cent and were well over a million dollars short. In the weeks leading up to launch, we raised a private round for $200,000, a convertible note for $200,000, we hit our $400,000 crowd-funding target, and a major bank finally came to the party and loaned us $800,000.

We lived to fight another day. Barely. If that risk isn't obscene, I don't know what is. This is my thirteenth year as an entrepreneur, and the risks are only getting bigger.

But these are very minor risks in the grand scheme of entrepreneurship. Just look into what some of the super successful entrepreneurs have had to do to get to that level of success. Elon Musk's story is well documented, spending all of his $165MM earned through the PayPal sale on two new businesses only to find himself in a position where both were within weeks of catastrophic failure. Only a few freak events in the space of a few weeks saved them, and he went on to launch a Tesla Roadster into space and become the poster boy for modern-day entrepreneurship. Imagine what would have happened if SpaceX didn't get the NASA contract and Tesla didn't get the government funding to get them through the Global Financial Crisis. Elon would have gone from a man worth $165,000,000 to someone bankrupt and looking for a job.

No normal sane person would take risks like that, but these are the risks that entrepreneurs take. And that's what makes them entrepreneurs.

STOP PERMISSION
SEEKING

The number one reason why entrepreneurs fail is that they aren't really entrepreneurs. An entrepreneur is someone who forges their own path in the face of obscene risks, increasing uncertainty, and very little support. This is not a job for everybody. It's a job for 1% of 1% of people. It's for the weirdos, the ADDers, the people who prioritize achievement, fun, and change over the reality of making life work on a daily basis.

Entrepreneurship is for people like Steve Jobs and his famous "reality distortion field." It's not for people who constantly seek permission and people who value approval over all else. In fact, it's the exact opposite. Yet, that is the vast majority of activity I see in the entrepreneurship space: seeking permission and valuing approval.

In my private Facebook mastermind group this week, one member proposed a new name for his project. It was filled with cliches and generic hip business terms like "freedom" and "lab" and "collective." Two people responded suggesting a new word to consider in the name, and from then on, the entrepreneur felt validated that it was the right approach.

What a fucking awful way to forge your own path. Steve Jobs would turn in his grave. You think because two people in a Facebook group like a word, that this is the direction you should go?

This gross overvaluation of approval has to stop if you want to be an entrepreneur. Here's a better idea. Deeply study the problem, the solution, the points of difference, the personalities of the founders, the market, the other products, the timing, and all other key factors. Deeply study design and follow designers, pay attention to how artists use metaphors and abstract interpretations to create new things from loose links. Look at other startups, study their names, and look at their branding. Look at companies who are recently successful, and look at their colours, their image, their social media accounts, and the sort of models they use. If you must ask your friends, then ask your friends, but only to form one-hundredth of one-hundredth of the data you use to make your decision. After all of that, ignore all of it and pick a name that sounds good.

You will be streets ahead of 99% of entrepreneurs with this approach. You will not only be refusing to follow boring, overdone cliches, but you will be doing something far more important—deciding for yourself. Right or wrong, the ability to decide for yourself is central to being an entrepreneur. Moving forward in the face of uncertainty is your reality from now on. No one knows the answer; no one can give you permission. It's on you.

DON'T BE TOO DIFFERENT

In July 2006, I left my comfortable and successful corporate career to start a business making websites. In the first week, I met up with a business coach who grilled me on what was going to be different about this business of mine.

From that day on, I was obsessed about being different. Indeed, one of the first things you will learn in business school is the importance of having a competitive advantage. Entrepreneurs, in general, are obsessed with being different, but it took me a long time to realize the dangers of being different.

These days, I have a much more stable and traditional business, and I have the job—for the sake of shareholders, staff, and founders—to keep it alive. The craft beer scene in Australia is exploding, and there's no shortage of companies wanting to get into the scene.

I'm approached regularly from startups wanting to work with us to get some exposure for their product, everything from pour-at-home beer systems to beer in wine casks to apps to engage our customers at the taproom. One thing I've come to realize is that it's only the very boring ideas that actually get through and end up becoming suppliers of ours. Grain producers who can offer slightly lower shipping costs or photographers who have a slightly different portfolio of work or shirt printers who can also print bar decals and coolers on the same order. In other words, having some small point of difference is important, but the ones who are in entirely new territory I will stay well away from. I don't want to be the one risking our business reputation on some unproven idea. A cask of beer is not something I need, so why would I put our brand on one.

Along the lines of what I said in my first book, *The 7 Day Startup*, looking for problems where people are already paying for solutions and tweaking them slightly is usually more fruitful than inventing something completely new and trying to convince people they need it.

In the past, when I've worked on original business ideas, I've become excited that no one else seemed to have thought about this before me. I see this all the time in entrepreneurship groups as well. It's seen as a good thing that this great new idea you have is not already being done by someone else.

The truth is that, except in the rarest circumstances, it's actually a bad sign. If no one has thought of it, it probably isn't wanted. Trying to make something wanted is a monumental task.

I've learned this many times, the most recent being with our core range of beers. We had a great idea for a beer that bordered on a new style of beer. There was an existing style called Farmhouse a champaign-like Saison-style beer that was well established. We wanted to add some new world hops to offer a modern take on the beer. Our brewery was on the coast, so we were taking the old Belgian style and adding in some more beachy elements by way of the new hops, and we called it Beach House. It was a stroke of genius by my best mate and Black Hops co-founder, Eddie, and more genius by my other co-founder, Govs, who created the beer exactly to spec. It's our favourite beer. It's won a gold medal at the last two Australian International Beer Awards (AIBAs), and it was our flagship beer when we launched the brewery. It was the beer that we hoped would catapult us into the list of Australia's Hottest 100 beers, a fan-voted poll of the country's favorite craft beers. In the first year, we listened to the countdown thinking we had no chance. We came in at #113. Things were looking promising. We didn't make the list, but since they publish the secondary list, we could see that our fan base was getting behind us, and we were on the right track.

The following year, we pushed Beach House again, and we intently listened to the countdown. We weren't together on that day; I listened from my unit all the way from 100 onward. When we weren't in the first 50, I was an even mix of nervous and excited. I felt it was about an even chance we either weren't in the list at all, or we were in the top 50. We were only a small local brewery, but we had a vocal following, and I felt we were in a good position to make the list. I listened to the entire thing, and as we approached the top 20, I realized that we actually hadn't made the list at all. After all was said and done, we checked our result, and we were #118—worse than the year before.

I was devastated. Yes, it's a popularity contest, but I just felt that what people vote for is a good reflection of how much impact you are having with your product.

The next day, I went out for a beer with my mate. It was at a venue that sold our beers, and he ordered a pale ale from another brewery. He said to me, "You guys need a beer like this."

It was those two events that made me add pale ale to the agenda of the founders meeting for the next day. I argued we needed a flagship beer that was the kind of beer most craft beer drinkers wanted to drink, something that would not require people to think. We had great value with our brand Black Hops, and if people could see the words "pale ale" (Australia's most popular craft beer style) next to it, then we'd have the right mix.

On 27 January 2018, we once again joined together to listen to the hottest 100. This time, our worst fears didn't materialise. Our IPA (which was also not previously a core beer) came in at #55, and our Pale Ale came in at #20. Given our small distribution at the time, we were one of the stories of the day. In 2019, our pale ale came in at #14. It's the highest rated Aussie Pale Ale on the beer rating app Untappd, and it outsells all of our beers 2 to 1 or more.

If not for our creatively named "Pale Ale," our business may not exist today. No one walked into a bar and asked, "Can I please have the Saison?" As soon as we had a beer that represented a well-brewed, excellent example of a style most people were planning on ordering, our business exploded.

We were the victim of our own creativity.

What you want is a healthy market of people buying more or less exactly what you are selling. Without that, you are almost certainly going to fail, and unless you are ruthless in your failure, it will be a very long and excruciatingly painful and embarrassing process.

People buy what they are planning to buy, so don't be too different.

YOU DON'T HAVE TO WIN

There is an obsession in entrepreneurship about winning. Every mission statement I look at and every ambitious young entrepreneur I speak to wants to be the "biggest" or the "leading provider" or "the highest rated" or be "number one."

In any given field, the businesses still operating are already the winners. You are now comparing yourself against a small group of winners. Most companies have failed and don't even get spoken about.

In many ways, you've already won. But that's not why aiming to win is a problem. The main reason is that you probably won't.

Winning sounds great on paper, but in all likelihood, it will end up being a vision that never gets realized and therefore never provides any real value. Or even worse, it just serves as a reminder to everyone involved that you are losing. Great way to de-motivate the team!

The argument I guess would be to aim for number 1 and if you fail, number 2 or 3 ain't bad. But really, when you are starting from 0, numbers 1 through 20 are extremely good and also extremely motivating. Number 2 is astonishing if you started at 100 and have aimed for top 10. It's an abysmal failure if your heart is set on winning.

You've heard my story already about how excited our team was when we hit #20 in the Hottest 100 craft beers. Don't lose that magic! #20 at that time was amazing to us. If all goes to plan, we will be making a big push into the top

10 next year. What if we don't make it? What if we come in at #11? We'd be devastated.

When Pale Ale came in at #20, it was the highest debut entry to the list and the second highest entry from our state of Queensland. We took a photo in front of the wall, and it became our most-liked social media photo ever up until that point. Me, Eddie, and Govs, our staff, our customers, our suppliers, and everyone between were ecstatic at the result. It's amazing to think that such a modest goal would generate such attention, celebration, and motivation. And to also think that if next year we come in at #11, we'd be devastated.

Imagine if our goal was to win that list. We'd have, at best case, a decade of unhappy results.

Anytime anyone asks me about our vision for Black Hops as a whole, I never say I want to be the biggest independent brewery in Australia or the number 1 craft brewery in Australia. I think that's a bit unrealistic because we are up against some extremely good competition. Other breweries brew at 10X the scale of us, have investors with 100X as much money, and started their breweries decades earlier. If we can go from three mates brewing a homebrew in our garage to even knocking on the door of the top 5 in this industry, that's an insanely significant achievement. If we can have a brand that Aussie craft beer drinkers love, then that's great. More importantly, if we can stay in business and become a good contributor to the industry and the broader community, then that is a meteoric level achievement.

I don't believe there is any value to anyone in going after number 1. It would de-motivate the team, it would create years of unnecessary struggle and failure, and ultimately, it doesn't matter.

For most entrepreneurs, it's the same. They don't actually believe they have to be number 1, they just set that goal because that's the only precedent. It feels lame to set a goal of being number 2 or 3, but the sporting culture that's led to the fascination of being number 1 does not apply to entrepreneurship. Numbers 2 and 3, in most decent-sized industries, represents an extreme level of success that any entrepreneur should be ecstatic about.

Don't aim too high. Aim to improve your current position, but set goals that will motivate yourself, your co-founders, and your staff, and enjoy every step of the journey. You might find that going from #113 to #20 is far more satisfying than going from #3 to #2.

ONE DOES NOT SIMPLY "MAKE" LUCK

One of my favourite useless entrepreneurship sayings is: "You make your own luck." No one wants to admit that some factors are out of their control. That's especially true for people selling you solutions. Can you imagine signing up for an info product that tells you that you just have to be lucky? That will never work, so people dismiss it with statements like "you make your own luck."

But you can't "make" your own luck. If you made it, it would be execution, not luck. And besides, just like "work hard," it doesn't explain why so many people are working on their businesses for so many years and not achieving success. There are shitloads of people working hard or working on making their own luck, but for whatever reason, they don't get lucky. Perhaps it's because luck tends to be a bit random. That's the whole point of luck.

To me, it's okay to admit the truth that luck has a big role to play in success in business. It keeps you humble. As soon as you think you are entirely responsible for your success, you become arrogant. It's happened to me a few times before crashing back down to earth as soon as my next idea fails.

How did Elon Musk become the god-like figure of entrepreneurs? Sure, he worked hard and took obscene risks, and he's stupidly smart and creative. But like we talked about before, he was within inches of it all being one big devastating failure. In 2008, he was within days of bankruptcy, and he landed a huge contract with NASA that saved his space exploration company, SpaceX, and was granted hundreds of millions of dollars from the government to keep his fledgling electric vehicle startup, Tesla, afloat. I'm sure over decades as an entrepreneur that he's had his fair share of bad luck. But let's be honest, that series of events is nothing but good luck!

Every entrepreneur I know, including me, has a similar story, albeit at a much smaller scale. Some choose not to admit to it because it's a hit on the ego. People who have enjoyed some success have, more often than not, had a very well-timed strike of good luck.

That's part of the reason I'm always wary of taking advice from people who are monetising that advice. They will never acknowledge luck, so how honest is their advice really? Even those who aren't monetising the advice are still very unlikely to recognise luck as a major factor. Their egos and their self worth are on the line. It takes a lot of honesty and self-reflection to acknowledge the role of luck.

But it's there. The elephant in the room. It's always there and is arguably the main dividing line between moderate and extreme success in business.

I say embrace it. Don't let your ego get out of control if you do have some success, stay humble, and be grateful. And if you haven't yet, maybe it can help to think that one tiny, unpredictable event can change everything. There's room for a tiny bit of magic here, right?

IDEAS MATTER—A LOT!

I'm sick of hearing business experts claim that ideas don't matter, only execution matters. This is some of the most damaging advice an entrepreneur can take on.

It's basically saying, "Don't worry too much about what you are working on; just keep working." The problem is, this is the biggest problem we have: working too hard on the wrong things.

If you believe this advice, how do you know when your idea sucks? And believe me, some ideas suck; in fact, most of them do. Most of mine, anyway.

At the time of writing this, Apple is the most valuable company on earth after recently passing the trillion-dollar valuation mark. There was a time when Apple was not worth much at all. It was after a long stretch of bad ideas, products that missed the mark, and a lack of innovation after losing its spark. Their epic comeback came off the back of a bunch of great ideas. Your whole music library in your pocket—great idea! A computer in your pocket—great idea! They would not even exist right now if not for these ideas. Of course, they were well executed, which is equally important. But it's executing the great ideas that created the value.

One of the things I've struggled with the most as an entrepreneur was continuing to bust my arse working on the wrong things. Only after a long, painful period was I able to see that all of the wasted time, sleepless nights, stress, and anxiety were for nothing. Why? Because I was working on bad ideas, and I was no good at figuring that out quickly.

Please don't fall into the trap of the modern "hustle at all costs" Instagram entrepreneur and completely de-value the concept of a good idea. Our society, our history, our whole existence comes off the back of good ideas. Working hard is a prerequisite, but work hard on a good idea.

BE NOWHERE

When I was starting out in online entrepreneurship, there was a very popular phrase around the community: Be Everywhere. It was coined by Pat Flynn, a super nice guy and one of the early poster boys for Internet marketers. I thought a lot about this advice. I recall it kind of made sense for Pat Flynn because he was, well—Pat Flynn. Everyone knew who he was, so it sort of made sense to spread that as much as possible. But he wasn't giving the advice to Pat Flynn; he was giving the advice to every other new entrepreneur who followed him.

One of my favorite things to do is to review websites. I've reviewed thousands of them. The most fun I ever had reviewing websites was when Pat Flynn and I crossed paths. He was generous enough to have me on his podcast, and at the end of the episode, I thought it would be cool to offer a website review to everyone in his audience. I ended up doing hundreds just from that one post!

But looking back, I'm a bit regretful at never offering potentially the most useful piece of advice on someone's website. That is, to delete it.

Distraction is the enemy of any kind of progress as an entrepreneur. Not only is your limited time, energy, and money wasted, but so is the opportunity you gave up for working on the wrong things.

In this day and age, distractions are at an all-time high. We are bombarded with thousands of messages in dozens of formats in every aspect of our lives. When it comes to business advice, the idea of "be everywhere" has consumed new entrepreneurs to the point of stagnation. With limited resources, you cannot possibly be everywhere nor should you be.

Social media platforms are coming and going at a pace that has never been seen before. And with each emerging platform comes a tidal wave of advice that says "you must be on x." At a recent business event I was at, one leading entrepreneur proclaimed, "I'm creating hundreds of pieces of content per day. I should be creating thousands, and so should you!"

This entrepreneur is very good at social media and always has been. His business relies heavily on it, and it's his main source of marketing traction. So for him, it's good advice to do more of what's working and what's always worked. But what about for everyone hearing his advice? It's a huge leap to assume that what's right for someone who had proven they can make tens of millions of dollars from their online content is also right for a new entrepreneur who has no proof.

The problem is that not all work is recognised. Great work is often recognised, but it's not always recognised, and it can take a long time.

I say be nowhere. Trying to be everywhere is damaging and stressful and setting you up for failure.

Be nowhere unless you feel like it's a place you can do your best work.

It's not possible to be good at anything while doing everything. Or said another way, it's not possible to do great work anywhere while being everywhere.

This section will require some serious self-awareness. I will tell you right now, no one is going to tell you that you suck at a certain type of marketing. You have to figure that out for yourself.

If you are a boring and nervous speaker, you shouldn't take up public speaking because your business coach says it's the best way to build authority. Being a shitty public speaker is a great way to lose credibility. You have some soul searching to do. Anyone can speak at an event, but at every event, there are one or two speakers who stand out. Just like in business, a few stand out, and the rest are mediocre.

How can you stand out? For starters, you want to do some speaker training, probably weeks' worth, to really understand the complexities of public speaking. You want to learn about NLP and the best way to communicate to influence. You want a great design brain to make sure your slides work. Not just slides filled with info but a clean, crisp design that matches the presentation and doesn't distract from it. On that point, you want to study stand-up comedy because timing is everything. Figure out what individual words to use instead of others, group things in threes for maximum effect, and time slide transitions for a reaction.

You want to consider your place on the stage and limit the number of unnecessary movements.

You want to position yourself at certain places on the stage to reflect your story. On that point, you want to learn the art of storytelling, writing, and marketing to refine your message into something people will believe in.

You have to dress right and make the audience feel like you've got the answer.

You want to know what position to hold your hands in depending on what topic you are discussing or what interaction or response you are expecting from the audience. You want to learn to stand without being aggressive or submissive or too relaxed but confident.

You want to learn where to place things in the room and where to signal when you make points to subconsciously drive the audience behaviour. You want to work out what words to put around the room or on your slides to hone in your message. You want to learn the best microphone and stage setup to use and what words to use when you test them to show you are relaxed but confident and an authority.

You want to learn the right words and approaches to use for audience interaction to make sure people are encouraged to ask questions but not to expect their life to be changed by your answer. Don't get me started on how to change up presentations between events or how to manage tech failures or what fonts to consider for your slides or how to subtly sell from stage or what supporting stories to add or how and when to use swearing or shock—the list goes on and on and on. And believe me, those one or two speakers at your next event will know all of this stuff and a lot more.

I'm not trying to scare you into not creating things. My last book, *Create or Hate*, is there if you are in a creative rut, and it will motivate you to make things because ultimately that's what successful people do. However, don't make all the things. Make things well. If you are up for the challenge of public speaking well or podcasting well or making YouTube videos well or writing books well or running an Instagram account well, then go for it.

But you cannot do everything well. You can not "be everywhere" well.

So be nowhere; delete everything. Do nothing unless you can do it well.

.... TRUMPS QUALITY

The quality of everything you do matters, but there's something that matters more.

If you look at any recent business success and try to pinpoint it to a quality metric, it won't work. Every time you try, you will find countless other businesses doing things better, but for whatever reason, less successfully.

This used to frustrate me as an early entrepreneur. I'd try to get better and better at blog posts, but the CopyBlogger posts would go viral, and mine would go unnoticed. I'd try to build better and better websites than my competitors, and I'd struggle to gain new business.

In the end, over years of struggling businesses and ideas and marketing efforts, I have only had two that have gone well. And I honestly can't say exactly why. For whatever reason, my WordPress support business took off and so did my brewery business. And while I was a bit slow to react in some cases, I ultimately came around to an idea. That idea was the quality of everything else I was working on didn't really matter that much; what mattered was that this other idea was taking off.

This can be a hard thing to navigate. You can work years on something only to find that for whatever reason no one cares. Then you can spend minutes on something else, and it can take off.

Some people say doing the same thing over and over and expecting a different result is the definition of insanity. I say it's a better definition of entrepreneurship than the one offered by Merriam-Webster. Sometimes, results aren't perfectly predictable.

Sometimes, things just work, and sometimes they don't. I encourage you to do great work, but I suggest that if you want success as an entrepreneur and the path presents itself where you don't expect it, you should follow.

It can be tricky to navigate attention because a lot of it can be short-lived. But this is one of the skills you need as an entrepreneur. You need to be able to recognise traction and realize that you might be wrong. Traction trumps quality.

DON'T TAKE ADVICE *ON* BUSINESS FROM PEOPLE WHO ARE NOT *IN* BUSINESS.

If you accept that success in business comes only after a healthy dose of luck, then the idea of a lifelong business guru should be troubling. I see it all the time; people who started a well-known business thirty years ago are worshipped as if they were gods.

I can't tell you how many times someone has decided not to take a course of action because some guy who had a decent business thirty years ago advised against it.

This is an extremely fast-evolving environment we are in, unlike anything we've seen before. Taking advice from someone who isn't doing great things *right now* is a bad idea. The problem is that most people doing great things right now are not in the business of giving advice.

But the game has changed. The people have changed. The rules have changed, and before they become rules, they'll change again. There are no rules!

I don't think you should look up to any business gurus. This is especially the case for ones who haven't been in the game for decades. The problem is that you tend not to be taken too seriously until you have been in the game for decades.

I remember when I worked in a co-working space there was an "office hours" type arrangement outside my fishbowl section where once a week a business expert would come in to give advice to the potential startup founders. The absolute drivel of awful advice I heard on the other side of that glass was frightening. Meanwhile, I was right next door building a million-dollar business from scratch using technology that wasn't even close to existing when those experts were last in business.

This is an actual post from a Facebook group in response to a question about the most important things for a new business to do.

"A well thought out Business model and thought out strategic business plan. Forcasting (sic), information systems (sic) model for your area of choice, income and expenditure model, staff training or outsourcing staff skills, internal and external security profile, supply chain security, logistics feasibility study. If manufacturing business..."

Sorry, I'm going to stop it there and point out that this person so far doesn't even know what industry this business is operating in, yet he's decided he knows exactly, document by document, what needs to be done. Let's continue.

"...input, processes and output feasibility, negotiating and buying skills, no fear of failure, learn from failure, Resilience (sic). To name but a very few. I'm now 70, been there done that got the T shirt and taught it at university level..."

It made me physically ill to read this. It's the absolute exact opposite of what startup founders should be doing in this day and age. That's the kind of advice you get from someone who had a business once and thinks they have all the answers.

You are far better off to observe current entrepreneurs' behaviour than to take specific advice from has-been entrepreneurs. The best thing about observing is you don't observe expecting answers. You just observe on the off chance that you might learn something. But you don't delegate your only job as an entrepreneur, which is to make your own decisions about your business.

Don't take advice *on* business from people who are not *in* business.

STAY IN YOUR
(COMFORT) ZONE

Perhaps I spend too much time on social media, or maybe I just follow the wrong accounts. It seems that almost every day I'll see another generic quote about fear and a trail of supportive comments that inevitably follow. Yesterday's was, "Everything good is on the other side of fear."

Almost universally, entrepreneurial experts will tell you to "face your fears" and "get outside your comfort zone."

The truth is that there's a lot of bad stuff on the other side of fear as well. That's the whole reason fear exists. One of the most damaging and dangerous things as an entrepreneur is stress and anxiety. I've been so stressed at times that I didn't even realize it was causing all sorts of crazy physical reactions in my body.

Once you have clear physical consequences of stress like severe pains, muscles ceasing to work, and panic attacks, you realize just how dangerous it is. I don't really think we should be encouraging it in every instance for no good reason.

I used to live by this advice. Like many people, I have a huge fear of public speaking. I decided it was the right thing to do to tackle it. A few years ago, I began to start speaking at business events. I took a speaking course, wrote entirely new and original content for each talk, and rehearsed my talks religiously. After each presentation, I'd briefly feel great, and then the fear of the next talk would creep in. Before talks, I'd be corrupted by fear. I'd be rude and abrasive and stressed for days or weeks on end. I'd live in fear of the next talk, which of course would inevitably go well, and then I'd repeat the process again. The five minutes after each talk I'd tell myself it was worth it.

My last talk was a keynote speech in front of 700 paid members at a business conference. As usual, it went well, and I was praised. But when I was asked to speak at the next event, I considered it a bit more carefully. Was it really worth spending the next three months stressing out and worried about this upcoming talk? What exactly would I get out of doing the talk? If I didn't do the talk and just spent the time working calmly on my business, would that be a better outcome?

After careful consideration, I decided not to do the talk, and I haven't done one since. That was almost three years ago.

Does that make me a failure for not overcoming my fear? Maybe it does, but I'm an entrepreneur. I don't get paid for overcoming fears; I get paid when I successfully build a great business. And I get personal reward and satisfaction when

I successfully build a business. Sometimes, those rewards are far superior to the five-minute ego boost you get from a successful public appearance.

In the last two years, I've built the best business of my life, and when possible, I've tried to avoid too much stress in the process.

Most of the time your best work is done when you aren't stressed and fearful. A relaxed state with plenty of sleep and working deep in your zone is often where the best work happens.

There are certainly times when overcoming fear is the right step. If the outcome puts you in the position you want to be in, great! Go to for it; take the leap. But don't invite stress and anxiety into your life for the sole reason that you think you have to overcome a certain fear.

Sometimes it makes more sense to stay in your zone.

IT DOESN'T FUCKING MATTER

This last month signalled the start of my thirteenth calendar year as an entrepreneur. In that time, I have had one hell of a journey. From buying a whole garage full of Chinese balance bikes I couldn't sell to spending hundreds of thousands of dollars on failed software apps. Losing a house and 100% of my net worth from failing at one particular business in my early 30s. Starting a business on a whim out of desperation late at night and going on to sell it to one of the biggest Internet companies in the world. Turning a passion project homebrew into Australia's Champion Small Brewery and an insanely fast-growing multi-million dollar business in the process.

Entrepreneurship is such a crazy ride that I'd never say I've seen it all, but let's just say I've seen a bit.

I've also done a lot. I've done a lot of work. Early on, I worked tirelessly on my business plan and idea. I documented my competitive advantage and slaved over a marketing plan. I've built hundreds of websites—just for myself. At one point, I owned 200+ domains all with live websites that I held for SEO purposes.

I've scrapped 50+ business ideas and names and hundreds of logos and design ideas. I've written hundreds of thousands, maybe millions, of words on my blogs and in my books. I've spent so much goddamn time on Facebook it should be considered an addiction, spent hundreds on automated SEO software and automated Twitter follower software, years posting and trying to grow my Instagram following, and even more trying to grow my email list of 17,000 (which I recently scrapped).

I've lived in entrepreneurship forums and attended events and meetups. I've done hundreds of podcast interviews and been in some sort of press hundreds of times and tried and failed to get into hundreds more.

I've never really stopped to think how much of this "work" was actually useful.

I'm active in the entrepreneurship space, particularly among new business owners, so I see entrepreneurs every single day doing the same things. It's a constant barrage of: What should I call my business? How do I get more followers on Instagram? Which design do you like better? How do I rank in Google? And the list goes on.

Out of all the work I've done, and all the ideas I've come up with, and businesses I've started, I've only done two things that have ever worked. I started a WordPress support business offering unlimited support to people struggling with their website for a fixed monthly fee. No such service existed in the world, and it took off. I then started a business making beer with my mates.

Those two acts of creating a business off the back of a great product have transformed my life and turned around my otherwise unsuccessful career as an entrepreneur. Almost everything else did not matter.

Out of interest, just for this book, I dug into one Facebook group and pulled out the first five questions I saw:

1. What gets more reach on Facebook, pages or groups?

2. What accounting software should I use?

3. What's a free/cheap way to manage leads in your business?

4. What software should I use for invoicing?

5. Does anyone know how I can find some more information on financial planning?

I guarantee I could continue scrolling for hours and get more questions like these: Which design is better? Which name is better? How do you get leads on LinkedIn? Should I be on Facebook or Instagram? How do I rank higher on Google? Which colorshould I choose?

These "entrepreneurs" are a bunch of permission-seekers, and it really troubles me. Here's the answer to all of those questions:

It doesn't fucking matter!

None of these questions relate to the one problem that I would guess every single one of these entrepreneurs has and the only thing that is going to make a significant dent in the trajectory of their business—a great product.

Uber did not take off because they chose the right invoicing software. It took off because there were millions of people frustrated with shitty taxi service, and Uber did it cheaper, more reliably, more efficiently, and more elegantly.

Netflix didn't replace Blockbuster because they had a better logo. The Netflix logo is shit; it's red letters. It took off because it provided a much better product: more convenient, more engaging, cheaper, higher-quality, the list goes on.

The same is true on a smaller scale. I ran my agency for seven years, and it failed every year. I had hundreds of websites and at least five or six brand names for it. It did not matter. The agency failed because it offered a shit product. I built websites for people. Big deal. So did 1,000 other agencies in my city. It wasn't until I re-thought the agency model from scratch and came up with the unlimited support idea that I all of a sudden had a better product. It was interesting, safe (like insurance), and no one else was doing it. It became newsworthy and simple and scalable, and it took off. In hindsight, the name meant nothing, the logo meant nothing. It grew because it was a great product, and customers raved about it.

You can go back as far in history as you like and every successful business had this one thing in common. Yet, now we have all the technology in the world, and no one wants to use it to figure out how to make a great product. They all just want more likes on their Instagram posts.

No business ever failed to take off because they used Quickbooks instead of Xero or because they chose the wrong free CRM or because they chose logo A instead of logo B. The reason your business is not taking off is that your product is not good enough. Period.

It's not interesting enough, it's not cheap enough, it's not different enough, it's not useful enough, it doesn't solve a big enough problem for enough people, or it's just not good enough.

Focus on making a better product for your customers. All the other problems you've distracted yourself with DO NOT FUCKING MATTER.

JUST BECAUSE YOU CAN MAKE MONEY DOESN'T MEAN YOU SHOULD

Many times, over my years of being an entrepreneur, I've found myself in a position where I've started some line of business, not because I should, but because I could.

Two examples are selling content (things like online courses) and starting a membership. Over years of being active in Internet marketing groups and looking up to these types of entrepreneurs, I had it drummed into me that I was leaving money on the table not having a higher level online program or membership. Quite a few times, as a result,

I started such a program or membership as a result. Not because I saw a great business opportunity to offer something different and build a high-growth and high-potential business, but because it seemed like an easy way to make money, and it felt like I was leaving it on the table by not starting them.

But in all cases, these projects have failed. Not failed in the sense of not making money. I've made hundreds of thousands of dollars off courses and memberships. But failed in the sense that ultimately they didn't turn into a high-growth and valuable business or brand. Nor did they turn out to be a good expenditure of my time. And the reasons in hindsight are obvious. They were generic offerings with fleeting customer interest in an extremely over-saturated niche.

These days, I don't sell content, and I don't have a paid membership. I offer only free content, and I have a free membership. I actually cancelled the subscriptions of all of my paid members once I realized that what I was offering wasn't high enough value for them and wasn't interesting enough as a business to me. The only exception for me is my books, which I would happily give away for free except you have to charge for books if you want to be in the main Amazon bookstore (which results in more people reading them).

If you are following a lot of the online marketers like I used to, you might be tempted to start a business selling online courses and memberships. This is cool if you want this style of business, but for me, entrepreneurship has always been about doing something big. I can't see the value in taking on all of the risks and struggles only to replace an average salary and have the ability to work from home.

Selling content directly, to me, is a lost opportunity to do something big. The idea has never sat that well with me because people don't like paying for something that they know they can get for free. It turns an otherwise legitimate commercial operation into a charity exercise.

Even businesses like the local paper, whose entire business is publishing content, still struggle with the idea of how to charge. Every fifth link clicked on Twitter goes to a paywall. That doesn't really seem to be in the spirit of modern content sharing.

To me, content is the perfect tool for marketing, not as the product itself. If you have to sell your content, I suspect you haven't figured out how to use it as effective marketing for a good business.

In my 2015 book, *Content Machine*, I defined content marketing as:

> "Releasing something interesting that grabs attention for a business and builds trust."

I also introduced the idea of monetization logic. That is, do you have a nice neat link between your popular content and some kind of product or service people can pay for. In other words, does it make sense that someone would consume your content and then dig in further to purchase your products or services?

And taking that further, can those products or services be built into a high-growth and valuable brand?

That's where the sweet spot is. High-value content given away for free drawing the masses into a high-growth and high-value brand.

Ignore the short-term urge to make money just because you can. Leaving money on the table means your content is even more valuable and your trust levels will be even higher.

With a decent business behind the content, the short-term sales of a $200 online course will seem like nothing compared to the potential to build a truly valuable brand.

WHAT IS YOUR VANITY
METRIC OF CHOICE?

I was at a business event recently, and the format was that the winner of each award category would be announced and they would be briefly interviewed on the stage.

The host had a few go-to facts about the business to ask about to impress the audience, and it worked.

When the winner of the influencer award got to the stage, she was asked about her approach to getting millions of Instagram followers.

When the winner of the marketing agency award was questioned, he was asked about his

expansion plans into offices in New York and
London.

The retail award winner was asked how she
was able to go from 0 to 800 staff in 3 years.

The usual "just go for it" and "back yourself"
and "be yourself" platitudes were offered, and the
crowd ate it up.

It's clear that each of these businesses had
one metric that they had chosen to focus on.
One metric that gave them a sense of pride and
achievement. One number that proved that they
were "killing it."

I thought to myself, *This is kinda stupid.* I
mean, for starters, I've built a seven-figure business
with virtually no social media presence, so I'm not
that impressed by numbers of followers. I have no
desire to have offices overseas, I love being close
to home, and there are endless opportunities right
here in Australia, so the number of overseas offices
doesn't mean a lot to me. As for having 800 staff,

fuck that! We have 15 and managing the team is a full-time job! (P.S. I love my team, so on the off chance one of them read this, you're amazing.)

But the truth is, I'm guilty of this exact thinking, and the evidence is in the first sentence of the last paragraph. Did you catch it? I'm so proud of building a "seven-figure business" that I made it part of the subheading in one of my books!

I've always been obsessed with revenue numbers. My first business goal after reading, *Think and Grow Rich* was to start a six-figure business. Once I did that, my next goal was to start a seven-figure business. I even blogged about my progress each month in income reports where I publicly published my revenue. Now that I've built a seven-figure business and another multiple seven-figure business, my goal is to build an eight-figure business. I wonder what my noble goal will be after building an eight-figure business? Wait I know—build a nine-figure business!

I guess I'm saying that I'm as guilty as the next person when it comes to obsessing over meaningless and randomly-chosen vanity metrics that make me feel good. I've had many vanity metrics over the years, such as the number of social media followers, number of customers, and number of monthly website visitors. I even used to marvel at my Klout score of 57! (Don't look that up if you don't know what Klout is, and if you do, please don't tell anyone I said that.)

I've given up on most of those vanity metrics these days.

At the start of this year, I gave up on one of my most beloved vanity metrics, my email subscriber list count. I used to have it plastered all over my site: Join 15,000+ smart entrepreneurs. After winding back my personal brand and deciding to focus more on Black Hops Brewing, I decided to cull my list. I emailed my list and explained I was changing providers and they could opt in at a new location. Out of the 15,000, around 1,500

decided to opt into the new list on MailChimp.
This took my email autoresponder bill down from
close to $4,000/year to $0. And my first email sent
had 50+ replies, more than any email I'd sent in
the two years prior.

The thing I'd placed so much meaning on,
was in fact, meaningless the whole time.

And that's what these metrics are, meaningless. That is, until you decide to apply meaning
to them. There is no inherent value behind these
numbers. They are just things that entrepreneurs
decide are important to them.

Most social media influencers make hardly any
money because they are obsessed with the meaningless stat of how many followers they have. The
agency owner who is obsessed with having an office
in New York probably doesn't count how many
people he employs. The retail business with 800
staff probably doesn't know how many Instagram
followers she has. Because those numbers for those
people are meaningless.

The number of followers is important only to the social influencer because she's decided it's important. The New York office is important to the agency owner because he's decided it's important. The number of staff is important to the retail business because she's decided it's important. These entrepreneurs have decided to place meaning on these numbers for whatever reason, probably because in their circles these are the things that sound the most impressive and what other people place meaning on.

What is your vanity metric of choice?

Perhaps a better question is, what would happen if you refused to apply meaning to any of these vanity metrics and picked a metric with actual meaning?

While you are obsessing over a stat that makes you feel warm and fuzzy, you might be missing out on the good things that businesses can do. Businesses are a great vehicle for a lot of things.

What about giving you the freedom to do what you love. Are you measuring how good of an employer you are or do you get excited about your impressive headcount stat?

What about time flexibility. Does your business allow you to work six hours a day and spend your time on hobbies and being a better partner, parent, or friend? Or are you on your phone during family time trying to get a few more Instagram followers?

What about creating wealth to pay taxes to pay for services for the population and less fortunate. Are you celebrating how much tax you pay? Imagine if you won an award and the presenter said, "This year, you guys paid $400,000 in taxes. What an amazing achievement! Tell us about your plans to pay more taxes next year."

People tend not to celebrate the actual legitimate benefits to themselves and others that come from having a business. Instead, they cheer when their social followers go up or they hit their annual feel-good revenue target.

Forget your vanity metrics and get back to why you have a business in the first place and how it can be truly valuable to you and others. Measure that.

THE PURSUIT OF
UNHAPPINESS

I have to assume that if you are reading this book, and you've made it all the way to the end, you aren't entirely happy with your current situation. Maybe you are a new entrepreneur wondering what it would feel like to be a successful entrepreneur. Maybe you have had some success but idolize other big-name entrepreneurs and want to go to the next level. I guess there's a chance you were just hoping to be entertained, and if that's the case, I'm truly sorry.

Wherever you are at, unless you've built an eight-figure business from scratch, there is a good chance I've been in your exact place.

I remember so many years of seeking success like it was going to be some kind of magical game changer. Expecting it to not only change my day-to-day life but also change me, change how I feel about the world, change how I interact with the world. I think entrepreneurship has that appeal. It can cause big changes, which is great, but it won't change everything.

When I sold my last business, WP Curve, there was a month or two where it didn't feel real. The money hadn't landed in my account yet, and I was still very unsure whether it would go through. To GoDaddy, the amount paid was a small amount. But for me, it was a lot!

After my co-founder, Alex, mentioned the night before that the transfer should be coming through tomorrow, I was understandably restless the following day. I was in a shopping centre when the constant scrolling to refresh produced something different. I'd refreshed hundreds of times that day, so the fear of it being $0 and the excitement of it being a lot more had mostly waned. I was just about to get up to meet my friend, and I gave it one more refresh. As it loaded, it sunk in. It wasn't zero. The money had come in; the deal was done; it was real.

I can't say how much it was because of an NDA with the buyer, but let's just say this: It's not a lot by today's standards of wealth, but for someone who grew up in Logan, this was more money than I could ever imagine would be sitting in my bank account. And to see it written there on my banking app was truly something else.

This was my moment. I was rich. And it took a while to sink in. In these days of social media, all I wanted to do was share a screenshot of it. But you can't do that, that's bragging and unnecessary attention (and also would have breached the NDA). Plus, it would make me a wanker. It's okay to share your income reports when you aren't making money, but when you are, it's just showing off.

It was a weird moment. An important and memorable one.

But it passed very quickly.

After the sale, reality kicked in. What would I do next? What would I do with the money? I had grand delusions of starting some kind of electric vehicle company and a software company and something more fun. Or maybe I'd just spend the money and actually feel what it was like to not worry about money anymore after almost a decade of brutal entrepreneurship.

I thought about buying an existing company or becoming an investor. I played around with all of these options, but in the end, after spending quite a bit enjoying myself, I put all of it into a house. Before the sale, I was renting a unit for $540/week in one of the nicest suburbs in one of the nicest places on earth: Mermaid Beach, Gold Coast Australia. I bought a house in the same suburb, a few houses from the beach, my dream location. I couldn't quite pay for it all, so I paid for most of it and still had a bit of a mortgage. The mortgage repayments ended up being exactly $540/week.

Ironically, I ended up in the exact same financial position as I was before. Of course, I had the asset, but on the downside, I didn't have a business to pay me a decent wage. It was a real reality check to realize that next week would be more or less exactly the same as this week.

And guess what? My happiness levels didn't change a great deal. I have problems now, too. They are problems that most people with a bit of context would agree are not real problems, but they still feel more or less the same as the old problems. Day to day, I have shit to do and problems to solve. Some things are easy; some are hard.

Logic would say that you are engaged in this entrepreneurship thing because you aren't 100% happy with your current situation, and you want to improve your situation to the point of being happy.

I know for me this was the case. I didn't see myself as average. I wanted more, and I wanted to live a different life and create something great for myself. But ultimately, I assumed that whatever I created would make me happy.

Humans are very bad at working out what will make them happy. There's a Dan Gilbert TED Talk (and book) that's well worth a look on this topic. His experiments at universities show that, when given enough choice, students will ultimately make decisions that result in them being unhappy. They assume that certain choices will lead to happiness, but actually, they don't. Turns out, us humans are very good at visualising the future; we just aren't very good at doing it accurately.

I am two years on from selling my business to one of the biggest Internet companies in the world. A few years before that, I was within two weeks of being completely broke, unemployed, and looking for jobs. You would think my happiness levels would have experienced an unrivalled explosion in that time. But guess what? They haven't.

Turns out, selling my last business was just a step toward starting another one. I love the current one very much, but it's also very challenging, very stressful, very demanding—all of the things you'd expect from a great business.

The idea of just spending the money doing nothing or travelling around had very little appeal. I can say with 100% certainty that I would be even less happy if I took that route because it turns out, people like to work.

Today, I tried to buy something at a hardware store, and my card was rejected. I'm constantly conscious of my money; I'm often stressed; I often wonder what is going to happen if this doesn't work out.

I'm very far from where I thought I would be once I became successful. I thought I would be more like the successful entrepreneurs you see in the media: rich, happy, and accomplished.

But that's not me. And to be honest, that's not all that appealing to me. I'm an entrepreneur, and I'm grateful for that fact, but I'm also realistic.

Entrepreneurship is not easy. It's a constant gamble and a constant hustle.

This book is about entrepreneurs seeking validation externally. What concerns me most about that phenomenon is this relentless pursuit of happiness. The idea that all of the sacrifices you make now will hopefully lead to a happier future.

Entrepreneurship is a struggle. The bad news is that it's always a struggle. Your level of success doesn't dictate the level of struggle. In many ways, the more you succeed, the bigger risks you'll take, the more you will struggle.

Have a look at the *60 Minutes* interview with Elon Musk where he cries recalling how he almost lost everything with SpaceX and Tesla.

That was very shortly after he sold his company for $165MM.

After 12.5 years in this game, I often wonder why I do it. Why *we* do it. Are we crazy? Probably.

I can tell you one thing. Being a "successful" entrepreneur isn't all that different from being a struggling one. The struggle is constant, so don't put all of your eggs in the future basket. If you are pining for a time in the future where you are all of a sudden happy, you probably won't be.

In the best-case scenario, you will get some success, and as a result, you'll have more options. More places to invest your money. More properties that become attainable. More businesses that need investing. More friends that enjoy your support. The list goes on, and fundamentally, the biggest surprise is you still just feel like you. And if you expect to give your life to entrepreneurship and in the end become someone else, you're sorely mistaken. No matter how successful, how rich, or how many hair transplants, you will still feel like you.

This doesn't have to be a bad thing. You have every reason to be happy, grateful, and accomplished right now. You don't need some external metric to supply that for you.

Be happy now. Be grateful now. Regardless of your success, you will always be you.

WHAT IS THE ANSWER?

I hope you have enjoyed this book and the advice within. The problem with advice is that for most advice, there is an equally if not more compelling truth in the opposite.

The customers are rarely right. Most are clueless, and some are complete arseholes.

Don't believe the bullshit no matter how convincing it is. Most successful entrepreneurs are busy working. Think for yourself.

Sometimes things don't work, and that's okay. Give up. Move on. Try something else but don't fall in love with it. If something works, it works. Focus on what's working. Business can be easy.

Question everything. Your resident business guru doesn't have the answers, I don't have the answers, and heck, you probably don't have the answers, either. But you are the best person to try. You don't need permission. If you feel you do, then this book is your permission.

Don't get caught up narrowing your business ideas down to a scientific equation. If it works, you will know; you won't have to ask people. If you have to ask people, it's not working.

Don't blindly take advice. There is no blueprint for success. Sometimes, increasing your prices is the right move. Sometimes, it's not. There is always a trade-off. Sometimes, focusing on profit makes sense; sometimes, it doesn't. Sometimes, bringing on investors is the best thing you could ever do, while sometimes it's the worst. If niching down works, then great. If it doesn't, go broader. If perfectly targeted marketing is crushing it for you, then great. If it isn't, don't be afraid to create content for the masses.

There is value in embracing alternative ideas and fuelling the ultimate business decision-making machine—you.

Design, story, and brand matter. But your mates don't have all the design answers, and design can't be whittled down to a Facebook post asking them to pick their favourite. Design is your biggest job; take it seriously.

Don't envy failure. It's painful, it's not fun, and it shouldn't be celebrated. By all means, keep trying, but don't invite failure. The goal is to succeed.

Entrepreneurship is a risky endeavour; don't sign up for this if you aren't willing to take risks. But remember, with risk, there should be a possibility of a big upside. If there isn't, then what's the point?

You can't "make" luck. Accept that sometimes you will be fortunate enough to have it and sometimes you won't. Stay humble and grateful if you do, and stay hopeful if you don't.

Don't spread yourself too thin. Be nowhere unless you feel you can do it well. But remember, no matter how well you do it, traction trumps quality. Look out for traction.

Don't invite stress and anxiety. There is a time and place for going out of your comfort zone. But for the most part, stay in your zone. Do what you love and what you're good at.

Challenge your deeply held vanity metrics and look for something more. Don't desperately chase money. Build something great if you have the opportunity and fortune to do so.

The principles in this book have worked well for me. They may or may not work well for you. Ultimately, what has worked the best for me was to make the shift from being a student of entrepreneurship to being an entrepreneur. Business owners who desperately seek advice and permission from business leaders, experts, or celebrities are students.

Entrepreneurship, by default, is a position of leadership, so I encourage you to lead and not follow.

Don't idolize the future and expect everything to change. If you are healthy and happy, you are rich. A future version of yourself who is older, stressed, unhealthy, and with more money in the bank is nothing to idolize.

You have the opportunity to live your life as an entrepreneur, trying new things, taking risks and potentially making a difference in the world. That's pretty cool. There is a lot to be happy about and grateful about right now.

In case you haven't guessed it, there is no answer. And now is a good time to stop looking for one.